ing

100
Greatest Walks in
BRITAIN

INTRODUCTION

Assembling this selection of walks has served as a timely reminder of the extraordinary variety of walks in Britain. It's hard to think of anywhere else on the planet that can offer a choice of moorland and mountain, dale and downland, forest and coast in such close proximity. On many walks it's possible to mix and match landscapes to awesome effect, climbing from pretty villages into remote wildernesses, or yomping over rugged moorland to rollercoaster coastlines.

What's more, Britain is blessed with the finest mapping in the world and a footpath network second to none. The result is a countryside that makes it easy for walkers to access jaw-dropping panoramas, to enjoy grandstand views of spectacular events in the natural world, and then to finish the day with a celebratory pint in a character-packed pub.

The walks in this collection will guide you to fascinating places and magnificent views, creating memories you'll cherish forever. They're compiled by experts who know their patch like the back of their hands, and who skilfully link paths and tracks to make your walk as smooth as possible. Their insider knowledge allows you to explore beyond the usual honeypots.

A handful of the walks are easy, a few challenging, and the majority designed to be accessible to everyone with a passion for the great outdoors and a belief that Britain is better on foot. The combination of a clear route map and step-by-step directions make navigation straightforward. You don't need polar kit and a support team to do these walks; just a sense of adventure and an appetite for life. So make your choice, lace up your boots, and head out on one of Britain's greatest walks.

Jonathan Manning
Editor
Country Walking magazine

HOW TO USE YOUR
Country walking ROUTES

TIME An estimate of how long a route will take, based on a pace of about two miles per hour, with allowances for slower, hilly routes.

GRADES The routes are graded as easy, moderate or challenging, depending on distance, terrain, ascent and descent, and ease of navigation. Easy walks are generally short and relatively flat. Challenging routes require fitness, experience of the terrain involved, and confidence with map-reading.

ABBREVIATIONS
We have abbreviated left to L and right to R.

MAPS The orange route marked is the one to follow. Maps are based on Ordnance Survey Landranger 1:50,000 maps and each square represents 1km x 1km. It is essential that you take the relevant Ordnance Survey map with you (we recommend the Explorer 1:25,000 series) in case you get lost and leave the area covered by our map.

CENTRAL ENGLAND

1. **Herefordshire** Craswall
2. **Norfolk** Wells-Next-the-Sea
3. **Shropshire** Caer Caradoc
4. **Worcestershire** Malvern Hills
5. **Telford & Wrekin** Ironbridge
6. **Shropshire** Stiperstones
7. **Staffordshire** Chrome Hill & Parkhouse Hill
8. **Derbyshire** Tideswell (Monsal Dale)
9. **Derbyshire** Stanage Edge

10. **Nottinghamshire** Clumber Park
11. **Cheshire** Shining Tor
12. **Derbyshire** Bleaklow Bomber
13. **Staffordshire** Cannock Chase
14. **Derbyshire** Edale Horseshoe
15. **Worcestershire** Clent Hills
16. **Staffordshire** Roaches
17. **Staffordshire** Dove Dale

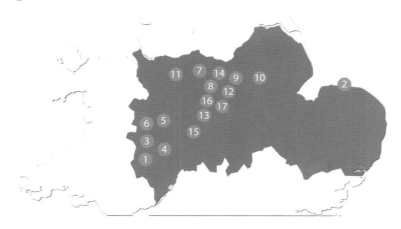

16

17

SOUTHERN ENGLAND

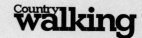
Country **walking**

SOUTHERN ENGLAND

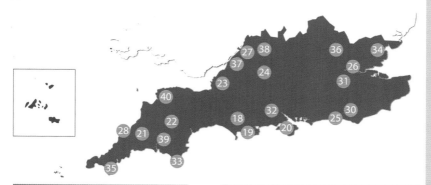

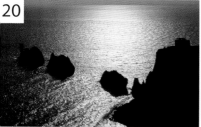

20

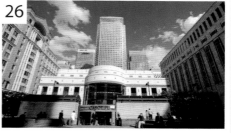

26

NORTHERN ENGLAND

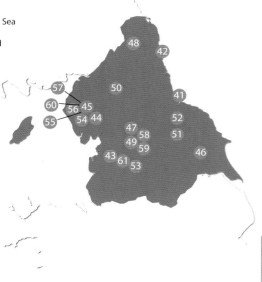

45

59

SCOTLAND

SCOTLAND

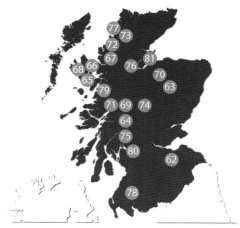

76

80

WALES

83

96

Country
walking

Distance	Time	Grade
12km/7¾ miles	3½ hours	Moderate

PLAN YOUR ROUTE

jurig • Clun • Ludlow
Knighton • Stou-
on-S
hayador
Llandrindod • Presteigne • Leominster
Wells • Kington • Bromyard
lth Wells HEREFORDSHIRE Gre.
Hay-on-Wye • Hereford
on-
• Ross-
Crickhowell • Abergavenny Glo
Ebbw • Brynmawr • Monmouth
• Vale • Blaenavon
Pontypool Lydney •
Bargoed Na
Cwmbran Chepstow

ROUTE

Is it for me? Upland peat moor, boggy in places, stony elsewhere; one steep descent; one long, stony bridleway with several fords
Stiles None
Suitable for most adults, children and dogs

START/PARKING

Bull's Head, Craswall, grid ref SO278360
Nearest town
Hay-on-Wye
Refreshments
Bull's Head
Public toilets
None
Public transport Nearest bus stop is at Peterchurch (Stagecoach 39/Yeomans 40, Brecon-Hay-Hereford, daily); on Sundays and bank holidays, May-Sept, Offa's Dyke Flyer serves the Bull's Head from Hay-on-Wye

MAPS

Ordnance Survey
Explorer OL13
Landranger 137

Near the southern end of the Black Hill.

Photo: Julie Royle

CENTRAL ENGLAND

Explore the wilder side of Herefordshire with this spectacular walk on the edge of Brecon Beacons National Park. The main feature is Black Hill, also known as Crib y Garth, and by some as the Cat's Back. Whatever you call it, this shapely little mountain is an offshoot of the Black Mountains and it's a great place to be. As you head south from the summit it narrows to a knife-edge ridge, its sheer eastern slopes plunging giddily down towards an English patchwork of small pastures, hedgerows and copses, its even steeper western slopes leading the eye across remote Olchon Valley to the formidable Welsh mountains beyond. Incidentally, the exact length of the walk will depend on your chosen

route – you can easily shorten or lengthen it, because this is access land, giving you flexibility. By Julie Royle.

❶ Start
Walk east along lane from Bull's Head for 100m then turn R on a bridleway. Follow to a T-junction and turn R. Turn L when bridleway rejoins lane, then join another bridleway at end of lane. This leads on to open, unfenced hillside and eventually intercepts a wide path (Offa's Dyke Path). However, you can bear L wherever you wish to meet this path somewhere below summit of Hay Bluff. Turn L.

❷ 4.5km/3 miles
Bear L on indistinct path, leaving wide path, which climbs over rounded top

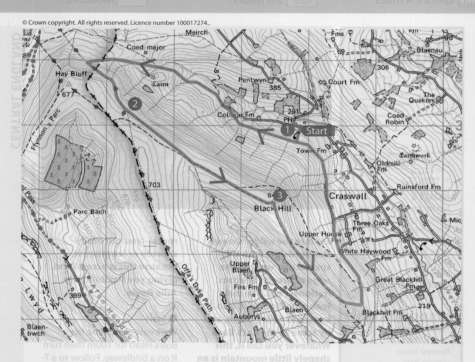

ahead. You're now close to highest point of walk (660m) which is also the highest point in England south of Yorkshire. It doesn't count as a separate top because it's part of Hay Bluff, the 677m summit of which is in Wales (though only just). The indistinct path soon becomes clear and you simply head south-east along ridge of Black Hill.

❸ 6.8km/4¼ miles
Black Hill's summit, at 640m, is marked by a trig pillar. Continue south, enjoying

increasingly excellent views as ridge narrows and becomes rockier, so that it's narrow enough for you to look down into valleys on both sides as you walk along. Eventually, you descend steeply to bottom of hill, avoiding car park which intrudes on this otherwise remarkably unspoilt place. Turn L on a bridleway which you follow for 3km. Turn R when you meet bridleway you used at start of walk and return to Bull's Head.

11.5 Distance 11.5km/7 miles	Time 3 hours	Grade Moderate

PLAN YOUR ROUTE

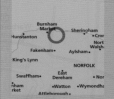

ROUTE
Is it for me? Mainly flat, footpaths and country lanes.
Stiles None
Suitable for most adults, children and dogs

START/PARKING
The Buttlands. Limited on-street parking. (There are paying car parks within Wells town), grid ref TF915434
Nearest town Wells-next-the-Sea
Refreshments The Three Horseshoes at Warham, various at Wells
Public toilets Wells
Public transport Norfolk Green Coasthopper daily, tel: 01553 776980

MAPS
Ordnance Survey Explorer 251

The quay at Wells-next-the-Sea.

A lovely walk in a beautiful part of Norfolk. It can be enjoyed at any time of the year. The walk goes inland to the tiny village of Warham and returns towards the coast where it picks up the coastal path to return to the start. By Alexandra Harrold.

❶ Start
Leave Buttlands by south-west corner (on the L diagonal from the Globe pub), walking down Plummers Hill to road. Turn L, then almost immediately R into Market Lane. Pass Alderman Peel School and bear L at cemetery to walk along green lane. Continue past farm buildings to Gallow Hill and Cuckoo Lodge.

❷ 1.75km/1 mile
Turn L, keeping Cuckoo Lodge R, and continue ahead along track to railway line. Cross line and turn L on to road. Shortly, turn R on to road signposted to Warham and continue along road to village centre and crossroads with Three Horseshoes pub, L. At this point there is an optional detour, totalling 2.5km, to Warham Camp, to see ancient earthworks of best-preserved fort in East Anglia. To visit, turn R down road signed to Wighton, follow road over bridge and take marked path, R. Retrace your steps to crossroads and Three Horseshoes, crossing road straight ahead into Chapel Street and continue as follows.

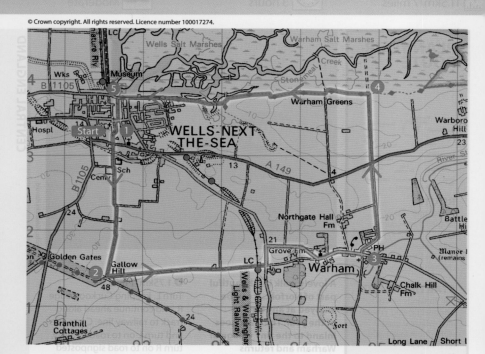

❸ 5.5km/3½ miles

Turn L into Chapel Street, which becomes Stiffkey Road further along. Continue ahead along road to A149. Cross to follow track opposite, Cocklestrand Drove, marked by a public byway fingerpost and continue along track, through metal gate and turn immediately L on to coastal path. This forms part of Peddars Way and Norfolk Coast Path.

❹ 7.5km/4¾ miles

Follow path all the way back to Wells, ignoring paths to L. If time and weather permit, pause to admire the view and rest on the seat, inscribed: "Syd and Twigg's favourite spot. Rest here and share the peace 1992." Path goes through some trees and when it emerges, bends to R. Stay on path which takes you through boatyards and along quay.

❺ 11km/7 miles

Turn L into Staithe Street, which is also signposted 'Shopping and Tourist Information Centre'. At far end of Staithe Street turn R and then almost immediately L to return to Buttlands.

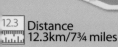

12.3 Distance 12.3km/7¾ miles	**Time** 3½ hours	**Grade** Moderate

Coming down Caer Caradoc with The Lawley in the distance.

Photo: Bob Atkins

CENTRAL ENGLAND

PLAN YOUR ROUTE

ROUTE

Is it for me? Tracks, quiet lanes, upland paths and access land; couple of steep descents
Stiles Several
Suitable for older children

START/PARKING

Church Stretton Railway Station, east side of railway, grid ref SO456936
Nearest town Church Stretton
Refreshments Cafés and pubs in Church Stretton; pub at All Stretton; tearoom at Carding Mill
Public toilets Church Stretton
Public transport Trains hourly from Cardiff and Manchester
Accommodation Book a B&B at the 'Book a Bed' section of www.countrywalking. co.uk

MAPS

Explorer 217;
Landranger 137

Explore access land on Caer Caradoc and the Long Mynd, with panormaic views to the Malverns and the Wrekin, the Brecon Beacons as well as Cader Idris. By Jenny Walters.

❶ Start
Take road from car park over A49 and Watling Street into Clive Avenue. Fork L down Snatchfield's Lane, then R on bridleway. Follow track to road, head uphill, and bear L along bridleway through gate. Go through farm, across field, into woods and through gate.

❷ 1km/½ mile
Turn L over stream, round hillside. Follow path through gate round to Hazler Road. Turn R towards Hope Bowdler and T-junction with B4371. Cross to bridleway opposite, through Gaerstones Farm and over stile, then turn R along fence to gate on to access land.

❸ 2.7km/1¾ miles
Bear R uphill towards Gaer Stone. At stone turn L and head NE over three summits. Continue NE, downhill to fence (don't go over), turn L down to gate at bottom. Take path rising to R, to woods and Cwms Lane. Turn R (ignore stile directly ahead), and over next stile on L signed Caer Caradoc.

❹ 5km/3 miles
Follow diagonal path over stile on R, and keep uphill, over another stile next to gate. Then turn diagonally L uphill on broad track. Follow to top, then turn R to walk along ridge to Caer Caradoc. Descend steep path to broad track and turn L. Follow down to fence, turn L on path beside fence to

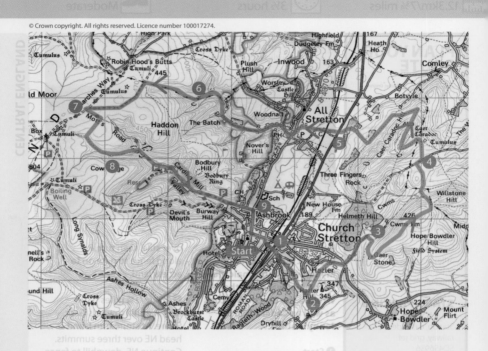

stream, and over stile on R. Go downhill over stile and through gate in R corner of field, L down track, then R across field to cross A49.

5 8km/5 miles
Cross field and railway, then bear L over stile to path between hedges. Turn R to footbridge, cross, and go over field to track. Turn L to B4370, turn L past Yew Tree pub, then R on lane signed YHA. Follow lane over cattle grid on to The Batch. Cross ford and follow track with stream, R. Keep following as path swings R

over stream and back to L along valley.

6 10.25km/6¼ miles
At junction of Jonathan's Hollow and Long Batch valleys, turn L over stream and follow track beside it, curving round to the R up Long Batch Valley. Follow stream uphill to cairn, and turn L on stony track to Marches Way.

7 12.5km/7¾ miles
Turn sharp L on Marches Way, heading SE towards Church Stretton. Shortly take green track on R, heading SW over

small summit, down to footpath contouring round hill. Turn L and follow to top of Light Spout waterfalls.

8 13.8km/8½ miles
Descend steep steps beside falls and turn L on path down Carding Mill Valley to car park and road. Follow road down past tearooms to T junction.

9 16.2km/10 miles
Turn R and follow to Sandford Avenue (the main street) and turn L. At far end, fork R into station car park and over footbridge to finish.

WORCESTERSHIRE
MALVERN HILLS

Country **walking**

3.5 Distance	Time	Grade
13.5km/8½ miles	4 hours	Moderate

PLAN YOUR ROUTE

Church Stretton · Bridgnorth · West Bromwich · Dudley ■ WEST MI
Stourbridge · Kidderminster · Solihull
Ludlow · Stourport-on-Severn · Bromsgrove
Redditch · Droitwich
iteigne · Leominster · WORCESTERSHIRE · Worcester · Pershore
ton · Bromyard · Great Malvern
HEREFORDSHIRE · Evesham
Vye · Hereford · Ledbury · Tewkesbury
· Ross-on-Wye · Stow-on-the-Wold · Cheltenham
enny · Gloucester · GLOUCESTERSHIRE
on · Monmouth

ROUTE

Is it for me? Moderately hilly with good paths and short turf
Stiles None
Suitable for most adults, children and dogs (on leads near sheep)

START/PARKING

British Camp Pass, below Herefordshire Beacon, where A449 cuts across hills, grid ref SO762403
Nearest town Great Malvern
Refreshments British Camp Pass and Wyche Cutting
Public toilets As above
Public transport Newbury Coaches 675, Great Malvern to Ledbury via British Camp Pass, Mon-Sat
Accommodation Book a B&B at the 'Book a Bed' section of www.countrywalking.co.uk mapS

MAPS

Ordnance Survey Explorer 190; Landranger 150

Just one of the views you can expect on this walk.

Photo: Julie Royle

CENTRAL ENGLAND

Edward Elgar was born at Broadheath, within sight of the Malvern Hills, which remained a source of inspiration. He later lived at North Malvern for a time, and then near Malvern Wells, and was never happier than when walking on the hills. By Julie Royle.

❶ Start
Take path to summit of Herefordshire Beacon, crossing British Camp then continuing south over Millennium Hill before descending a stepped path to a saddle. Choose path signed to Shady Bank Common. It runs along ridge top and is stony at first. When stones end, bear L on grassy path, skirting edge of woodland. Keep on in southerly direction when path forks, moving away from wood and gradually descending. Before long, Pink Cottage is visible below, R, at which point path swings eastwards, descending more steeply into woodland. Meet another path at T-junction, turn L and keep L at another junction. Descend to open common land to reach track which runs past farm (Dales Hall).

❷ 2.2km/1¼ miles
Turn L, beside hedge at first, then straight on when hedge moves away, following transmission lines for while. Pass Underhills Farm and Little Malvern Court to meet A4104. Cross, and turn L on footway, then turn R beside A449, soon passing St Wulstan's Church (Elgar's grave). Keep straight on at Upper Welland turn, then fork L on Holywell Road.

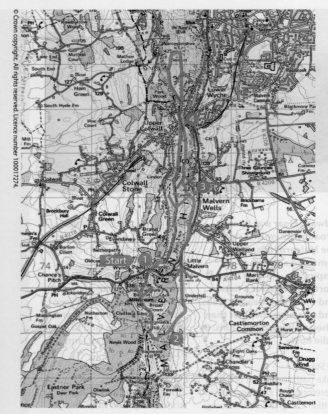

❸ 5km/3 miles

After passing Martell Mount take path on L which runs just above road for a while before climbing through woodland, following stream to a junction. Turn L, then R, so that you're on higher of two roughly parallel paths. At fork near green bench, take R-hand branch. Pass above Holy Well (an easy detour) then keep L at another fork by a green bench. Path eventually descends to merge with another, bordered by a wooden railing. Keep L at next fork, then straight on at another.

❹ 7km/4¼ miles

Turn L through Wyche Cutting, then R on Beacon Road. Climb over Summer Hill to top of Worcestershire Beacon, then return by any path (such as lower one on western side) to Beacon Road and the Wyche. Cross road to stepped path by bus shelter and toilets and regain ridge. Head south to British Camp Pass.

| 4.3 | Distance 14.3km/9 miles | Time 4½ hours | Grade Moderate |

PLAN YOUR ROUTE

The serene River Severn winds its way through Ironbridge.

Photo: Simon Whaley

CENTRAL ENGLAND

ROUTE

Is it for me? Disused railway lines, paths, bridleways and lanes
Stiles None
Suitable for older children; dogs on leads

START/PARKING

Dale End car park (long- stay £1), grid ref SJ666037
Nearest town Ironbridge
Refreshments Pubs along the River Severn – The Swan (01952 432306), The Malthouse (01952 433712), The White Hart (01952 432901)
Public toilets In car park beside Museum of Gorge
Public transport Tel: Telford Travelink 01952 200005

MAPS

Ordnance Survey Explorer 242; Landranger 127

Explore the gorgeous museums of the Severn Gorge World Heritage Site, before climbing gently through South Telford, glimpsing Madeley Court, a 16th-century Manor House (now hotel) before dropping back into the gorge through the picturesque narrow lanes of Ironbridge. By Simon Whaley.

❶ **Start**
From car park, turn R along road into Ironbridge, passing Museum of Gorge, R, then climb up to the Ironbridge. Turn R across this, then L into car park. Follow through to end, continuing on a wide track, waymarked as 'Severn Valley Way'. Follow disused railway line, pass sculpture on L, continue through gates,

under a road bridge and then a footbridge. Continue ahead through kissing-gate to Jackfield Sidings. Pass through metal gate, cross over road to continue ahead. Where road turns R, continue into Church Road, passing Jackfield Tile Museum, R, then bear L along road passing village hall, L, and church, R. At road end, join stone path along river, before reaching a junction. Turn L and follow drive as waymarked, then turn R on to stone path behind buildings, following to crossing track. (Bear R to visit craft centre.) Cross over, following building on R, then join lane, passing houses and Boat Inn. Follow lane round to R, then R again. Take signed path on L to rejoin disused railway. Turn L. Follow this to steps up to road.

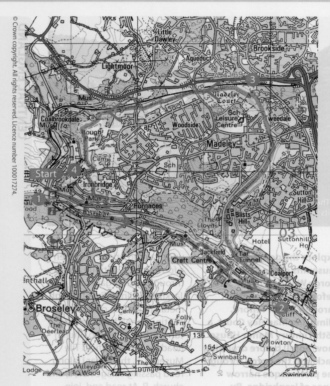

R through black gates, on to path with pond, L. Madeley Court can be seen, L. Follow bridleway, passing bridleway, R, to fork. Bear R, around playing fields, pass under road bridge, on to stone track through trees and fields. Cross over large crossing track and at next fork, bear R, then L to lane. Turn L, then R on to bridleway and follow, ignoring side tracks. After footbridge, R, take bridleway on L uphill into Oilhouse Coppice. Climb up to fork, bear R along field edge to marker post. Follow L-hand boundary, then cut across field to marker posts and follow good path around clump of trees, L. Path joins from L, but bear R at next fork, then through gateposts, with cemetery, L. Fork L and drop down to lane. Turn R, then turn L on to path opposite White Horse pub.

4 12.5km/7¾ miles
Continue ahead to kissing-gate and follow L-hand boundary to next kissing-gate. Turn R down lane, at junction turn L, then R into Belle Vue Road. Follow, but where this turns L uphill, continue ahead on path between houses, dropping to junction. Turn R down to next junction, then L down to main road. Turn R down to roundabout, continuing ahead to Ironbridge, then follow road back to car park.

2 4.5km/2¾ miles
Turn L, cross bridge and river, then turn L on to Silkin Way. Follow stone track to junction, turn L, then bear R on to smaller path around back of building, under bridge, and continue, signed to 'Coalport'. At crossing track continue ahead, signed to 'Blists Hill'. Path climbs gently, under Great Hay Incline bridge, later becoming concrete path with road down, L. Pass through tunnel, under two bridges, and

Blists Hill Victorian Museum on R, and continue climbing along road. Go over crossing track into park and at next junction, follow Silkin Way under road, bear R, across Station Road, following wide pavement over two roads. Continue straight ahead through trees on paved path/cycle track, to where it turns R, downhill.

3 8.5km/5¼ miles
Drop down, but turn sharp L on to path under bridge, then

Distance	Time	Grade
8.8km/5½ miles	3½ hours	Moderate

CENTRAL ENGLAND

PLAN YOUR ROUTE

Llangollen • WREXHAM • unde
Whitchurch
Ellesmere • Whitchurch
Oswestry • Wem • Market Dr
SHROPSHIRE Ne
Shrewsbury •
• Welshpool Telford •
• Montgomery Wolv
vtown Church Bridgnorth •
OWYS Stretton St
urig Ludlow l
Knighton • Stour
ayader on-Se
• Llandrindod • Presteigne
Wells • Leominster
• Kington

ROUTE

Is it for me? Long climb
to top of ridge; rough
stony path on ridge;
farmland and woodland
Stiles 3
Suitable for families with
older children

START/PARKING

Bog Centre car park, grid
ref SO357978
Nearest town Church
Stretton
Refreshments The Bog
Visitor Centre
Public toilets The Bog
Public transport
Shropshire Hills Shuttle
Bus service, www.
shropshirehills
shuttles.co.uk

MAPS

Ordnance Survey
Explorer 217;
Landranger 137

The Stiperstones ridge
from Nipstone Rocks
– see Point 1.

Photo: Jim Stabler

Walk along a ridge steeped
in history and myth, haunted
by Bronze Age burial cairns,
the Saxon warlord Wild
Edric, Roman lead miners
and witches. It's now a
wonderful nature reserve
and the furthest south that
you can find red grouse.
Listen to them, their
evocative call of "go back, go
back, go back" may be
warning you of the danger!
This is a wonderful family
walk with views that will pull
the eyes out of your head. By
Jim Stabler.

❶ **Start**
From start follow little lane
that heads south until you
reach Nipstone car park. Go
through gate and across stile
on your R and head up to
Nipstone Rocks. This area is
part of the 'back to purple'
project. Before this it was
hidden in trees.

❷ **1km/½ mile**
From rocks head east to gate
where you join Shropshire Way
long-distance footpath. Follow
path up through forest, across
to road and up on to ridge.
Take time to look back as
views are spectacular. Take
easier path to west of
Cranberry Rocks and walk past
Bronze Age cairns to highest
point of Manstone Rock with
its wonderful, precarious trig
pillar. Path hereabouts is rough
underfoot, so take care.

❸ **3.4km/2 miles**
Follow ridgeline past more
Bronze Age cairns and weird
rock formations to next large
outcrop of Devil's Chair where
it's reputed the devil can be
seen on dark and stormy
nights! If you walk path in
summer you will be
surrounded by whinberries
(the local name for bilberries).
From Devil's Chair path

Left: Manstone Rock, which you will encounter at Point 2.

descends to a small col with a cairn just before it reaches Shepherd's Rock.

❹ 4.8km/3 miles
From cairn follow track down to R where you leave moorland through a gate and cross into farmland. Walk past Hollies Farm where signposts point way to car park.

❺ 5.8km/3½ miles
Here walk changes character and as you contour hill you walk by side of old deciduous woodland alive with birdsong. Then it's on to an all-ability trail with benches that just demand a stop and a long look at the views. There are also 'wind-up' boxes that tell you all about the birds to be found here. All too soon this trail ends and you are at the Stiperstones car park.

❻ 7.5km/4¾ miles
From car park follow signs to Bog Centre and walk along road until you reach spot where you crossed earlier. Go back through gate and head for gate to your R. This is way down to car park where you started. Make sure you leave enough time to go to visitor centre. It will tell you all about the history of this once-thriving lead mining village. It also serves the best cakes and tea for miles around!

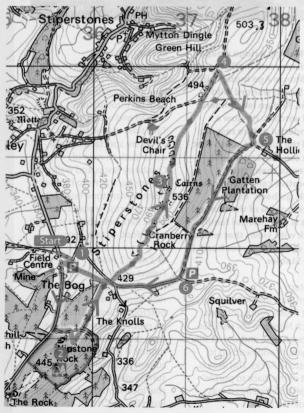

NOTTINGHAMSHIRE
CLUMBER PARK

 Distance 14.5km/9miles

Time 4½ hours

Grade Easy

PLAN YOUR ROUTE

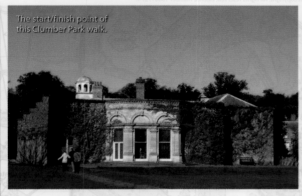

The start/finish point of this Clumber Park walk.

Photo: Alex Staniforth

CENTRAL ENGLAND

ROUTE
Is it for me? Mostly level
Stiles 1
Suitable for most adults and children

START/PARKING
Main car park near visitor centre and courtyard, grid ref SK625747
Nearest town Worksop
Refreshments Visitor centre
Public toilets Clumber Park and Hardwick village
Public transport Sherwood Forester bus 233 (seasonal)

MAPS
Ordnance Survey Explorer 270; Landranger 120

Owned by the National Trust, Clumber Park comprises nearly 4,000 acres of parkland, much of it attractive woodland. Once the seat of the Dukes of Newcastle it is one of the estates within the area known as The Dukeries and was begun in 1707 as a hunting park for Queen Anne. Unfortunately Clumber House was demolished in 1938, a victim of taxation; however, there are still many features for the visitor to enjoy. By Alex Staniforth.

❶ Start
From car park walk down to Clumber Lake via visitor centre and turn R along lakeside path through woodland, excepting a small conservation area, for 1km to Clumber Bridge. Cross bridge and take signposted

broad surfaced track ahead through woodland for 1.4km to South Lodge where, just before ornate metal gates (no access through), go L on signed path and around to join Freeboard Lane. Turn L along bridleway (part of Robin Hood Way) for 2.5km where just before A614 turn L along permissive bridleway in woodland to come to road leading to Drayton Gate.

❷ 5km/3 miles
Turn R, go through gate and cross A614 to take track opposite West Drayton Avenue, passing a plantation, Normanton Larches R. Keep on green track ignoring any side paths for 1km where open fields are met. Continue on for 500m where at footpath sign turn L up field by power lines for gap in woods ahead. Enter and after 300m bear slightly R

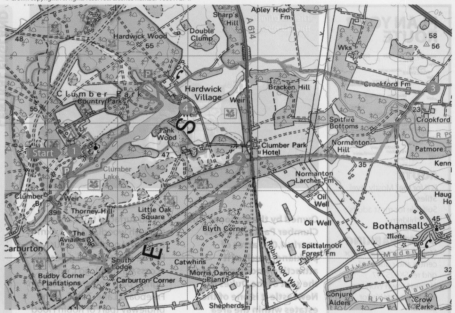

then L to pick up a wide track which proceeds to a ford across River Poulter. Cross via bridge and continue ahead uphill passing a bridleway on R to another bridleway on L.

❸ **8km/5 miles**
Turn along this, passing Crookford Farm, and over open fields – the woods on L are the curiously named Spitfire Bottoms. Continue forward on this bridleway passing through woodland to come alongside River Poulter again. Now

Clumber Park can be seen ahead. Continue on to A614 and, after crossing, enter woodland opposite. Pass through gate and follow path by wood's edge where at its end continue on field edge path 'til you reach minor road in Hardwick village. Go L down this road and at junction turn R going ahead to pass a toilet block. Exit L then turn R on to path alongside lake arm.

❹ **12km/7½ miles**
Follow path around lake

crossing a long causeway (foot traffic only) spanning inlet. On opposite bank turn L immediately taking lakeside path. Stay on this as it bears R along main body of lake then veer half-R leaving shore through trees, field and fence, L. Continue on to a gate under a small stone arch. Turn half-L along path through trees to lakeside. Go R along path which becomes Lincoln Terrace to return back to start, passing Gothic-style chapel and perhaps taking refreshment at visitor centre.

CHESHIRE
SHINING TOR

Country **walking**

2.1 Distance
12.1km/7½miles

🕐 Time
5 hours

👢 Grade
Moderate

The start/finish point of this Clumber Park walk.

Photo: Tom Bailey

PLAN YOUR ROUTE

[Map showing area around Manchester, Buxton, Bakewell, Stoke-on-Trent, Leek, Macclesfield, Congleton, Stafford, Derby, Staffordshire, Derbyshire]

Bolton • Bury   Hemswc
ATER MANCHESTER   Barnsley•
•Oldham Penistone•
Salford •MANCHESTER   Stocksbridge
is   •Sale Stockport •Glossop   Y
rincham •Cheadle
Wilmslow•   Whaley   Sheffi
•Knutsford   Bridge Dronfield•
Northwich   •Buxton   Ches
dlewich   •Bakewell   DERBYSHI
Congleton   Clay Cros
HIRE   Biddulph   Matlock•
e•   Kidsgrove Leek Wirksworth•   B:
wich •Stoke-on-Trent •Belper•
ewcastle-   Ashbourne
der-Lyme•
•Stone Uttoxeter   Stap
Drayton   STAFFORDSHIRE Derby•
•Stone   Burton upon

ROUTE
Is it for me? Clear footpaths, three miles of exposed ridge-walk, flagged paths over boggy ground. Suitable for reasonably fit walkers
Stiles 1 (on summit, to access trig point)

START/PARKING
Free car park at Errwood, on shore of Errwood Reservoir, grid ref SK014748
Nearest town Buxton
Refreshments Cat & Fiddle Inn on route
Public toilets None
Public transport Services to Goyt's Lane from Macclesfield and Buxton. www.traveline eastmidlands.org.uk

MAPS
Ordnance Survey Explorer OL24; Landranger 119

Discover the summit of Cheshire, here on the very cusp of the Peak District. This is a sensational walk with loads of variety, from the rhododendron woodlands of Errwood and the ruins of a powerful dynastic mansion to the spectacular views from the Shining Tor ridge, which take in everything from the Shropshire hills to the Bowland Fells. As an added bonus, there's a short detour to the Cat & Fiddle – Britain's second highest pub. By Nick Hallissey.

❶ Start
From car park, locate path running west, to R of information board. At fork, take R path and pass through a gap in low stone wall to enter woodland. Follow path past rhododendron and azalea bushes, descending slightly. At

waymarker, turn R on sharp angle, following sign for 'Errwood Hall'. Arrive at hall ruins and explore. Then seek path at north-western corner and continue into woodland, crossing boardwalk over marshy pool. At footbridge, do not cross but turn R uphill to reach waymarker for The Shrine and Pym Chair.

❷ 1km/½ mile
Follow this path along eastern slopes of hanging valley. Ignore path signed for 'Foxlow Edge' and continue on path, skimming top of plantation. After 2.4km, make short detour to visit Errwood Estate shrine, easily visible from path down a short track. Return to path and continue, emerging through kissing-gate on to narrow lane. Turn L and follow lane to brow of hill (Pym Chair), finding a kissing-gate,

➡

L, which leads on to Cat's Tor/Shining Tor ridge.

❸ 3.3km/2 miles
Go through kissing-gate and follow this clear path, flagged in places, across ridge. A grand view now opens up across Cheshire Plain. To south and west (on a clear day), you will see Clee Hills and the Wrekin in Shropshire, the Cheshire hills of Shutlingsloe, Beeston, Peckforton, Alderley Edge and Frodsham, as well as the Jodrell Bank radio telescope, and to the north the cities of Liverpool and Manchester, and Winter Hill in Lancashire. To the east you will see the Peak District, including the rear flank of Mam Tor and bulk of Kinder Scout. Continue on flagged path, eventually reaching trig point on summit of Shining Tor by crossing a wall-stile, R.

❹ 6.4km/4 miles
Cross back over stile and locate clear path veering south-east from summit, with a wall R. Follow to junction of paths and pass through kissing-gate. If a detour to Cat & Fiddle is not desired, turn L and descend direct to Errwood car park. To visit pub, turn R and follow clear path which leads to A537 Macclesfield to Buxton road. Turn L and follow for 220m to Cat & Fiddle Inn.

❺ 8.6km/5¼ miles
Retrace steps from pub back along main road and turn R to return to footpath. Follow track back to junction of paths encountered earlier, and follow path directly ahead, descending gently with Errwood Reservoir in sight. Ignore all branching paths and continue downhill, re-entering Errwood Estate and crossing a small meadow to return to car park.

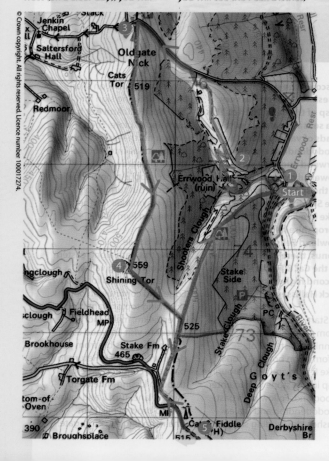

0.5	Distance		Time		Grade
	10.5km/6½miles		3½ hours		Easy

CENTRAL ENGLAND

PLAN YOUR ROUTE

ROUTE

Is it for me? Good forest tracks and paths throughout that take you into fairly remote country. Good waymarking where it counts. Watch for bikes in the forest. Suitable for most age groups – dogs on lead
Stiles None

START/PARKING

Whitehouse car park on minor road between Cannock and Rugeley. Parking area at junction of Marquis Drive and Penkridge Bank, grid ref SJ994161.
Nearest town Cannock
Refreshments Café at Point 5
Public toilets None
Public transport None

MAPS

Ordnance Survey Explorer 244; Landranger 127

Enjoy the good forest tracks and paths of Cannock Chase.

Photo: Steve Goodier

Cannock Chase is the last wilderness in the English Midlands and covers over 28 square miles of gentle hills and peaceful valleys where herds of deer roam freely. This route explores the Chase using good forest tracks and paths and following parts of the long-distance footpath 'The Heart Of England Way' to give an appealing circuit of this enchanting area. Do be vigilant for bikes as they are numerous on the forest trails. By Steve Goodier

❶ Start

Exit car park in L corner passing metal barrier to join good track that descends on to Cannock Chase. At marker stone with 'Bremen 25' on near picnic bench go R curving L downhill. Stay R when path forks and descend to T-junction of paths. Take good

track L and reach two sets of crossroads close together. At second (marker post 138) go R and follow track along Sherbrook Valley heading north. Follow this track for 3km or so ignoring any crossroads or paths leaving R or L and keeping small river on R. After L loop, track begins to enter woodland near head of valley to finally reach a clearing and crossroads of paths with stepping stones R over river to picnic area. Good lunch stop!

❷ 4.9km/3 miles

Go L uphill on bridleway to climb steeply. When track levels out carry on ahead ignoring any minor turnings L or R. When track splits go R and stay L when it splits again almost immediately. Continue to enter a parking area.

▶

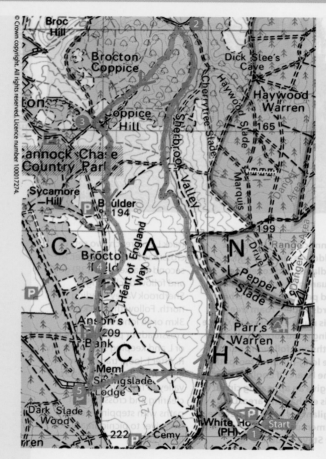

© Crown copyright. All rights reserved. Licence number 100017274.

❹ 7.9km/5 miles
Go R down car park and just before lane is reached take good path L signposted for 'Heart Of England Way'. Follow this across Chase passing a further car park, R, and finally descend through trees to reach parking area next to a white building on lane which is a café.

❺ 9.2km/5¾ miles
Go L up surfaced track just past café and walk up to higher car park. Pass wooden barrier ahead and take good forest track to reach double set of crossroads at entrance to Sherbrook Valley form outward route. At second crossroads go R, walk a short distance on good path and go L and uphill to climb steeply to marker stone ('Bremen 25') near picnic bench (also from outward route). Take path straight ahead and follow back to parking area.

❸ 6.1km/3¾ miles
Look for a track L as soon as you enter car park. Take this and follow to T-junction of paths. Take good track R to join another track at further T-junction, go L and L again at next junction to join the 'Heart Of England Way' footpath. Continue south on this towards communications mast and above Sherbrook Valley, L. Ignore turnings L or R until you finally reach major crossroads where you go R to descend to car park.

DERBYSHIRE
EDALE HORSESHOE

Distance 20.6km/12½miles

Time 7 hours

Grade Challenging

PLAN YOUR ROUTE

ROUTE

Is it for me? It's a full day's hike with uphill and boggy sections, but huge views reward your effort. Good navigational skills needed, particularly in bad weather
Stiles 4

START/PARKING

Car park in Edale (opposite station), grid ref SK124853
Nearest town Chapel-en-le-Frith
Refreshments Two pubs in Edale
Public toilets At start
Public transport Regular trains to Edale from Manchester and Sheffield. Call Traveline on 0871 200 2233; www.traveline.co.uk

MAPS

Ordnance Survey Explorer OL1; Landranger 110

On the Pennine Way leading up to Edale Rocks – see Point 3.

Photo: Tom Bailey

Bagging triangulation points is a sure way of guaranteeing good views. This route links four, all high above the beautiful Peak District valley of Edale; Mam Tor, Brown Knoll, Kinder Low and Edale Moor. It's a long day, but after the initial climb you stay high for miles and the views are sensational from start to finish. If you want to shorten it the route, take the Pennine Way back to Edale after trig point three. By Jenny Walters.

❶ **Start**
Leave car park by exit beside toilets and turn L on road to T-junction. Turn R, then quickly L on bridleway signed 'Castleton'. Walk past farm to path junction in woods, bear L on main track heading uphill, and on to gate on L just before

a house. Go through and turn R on path signed 'Mam Tor', up through gate on to access land, and on to another gate. Take stony track ahead, up to gate by road. Don't go through but follow narrow path to L of fence up to pass. Turn L to join stepped track up to summit of Mam Tor.

❷ **2.5km/1½ miles**
Follow steps back down to pass and road. Cross carefully and take path opposite up to ridge. Fork R on to footpath as slope eases (L is bridleway) and follow clear route straight on along Rushup Edge for over 2km until you reach signed path junction. Turn R for 'Edale via Barber Booth' and when main track swings R, take smaller L-hand path, past a post marker, and on uphill with tunnel airshaft off to your

L. Follow path in approximately north-west direction for over 2km (vague and boggy in places) to triangulation point on Brown Knoll.

❸ 8.3km/5¼ miles
From trig point, continue on path in north-west direction to fence. Cross stile and turn R on path down to track crossroads. Turn R through gate then L to join Pennine Way heading uphill. When path levels out briefly and forks, turn L up through Edale Rocks, past a cairn and on to a larger one, then head R to Kinder Low triangulation point.

❹ 10.5km/6½ miles
From trig point, return short distance to path fork and turn L along edge of escarpment. Continue past scattered rock formations of Wool Packs (path can be vague) and on to Crowden Clough. Follow across stream and on along edge, past a R turn out to Grindslow Knoll, to path junction at Grindsbrook Clough.

❺ 14.3km/9 miles
Turn L to follow path north along bank of stream, over it, back down opposite bank to edge, and on along escarpment for almost 2km to Golden Clough. A stony path

comes up from R – ignore this and continue short distance until you reach second one. Take faint path opposite (L) across boggy terrain to triangulation point at Edale Moor.

❻ 17.3km/10½ miles
From trig point, retrace route to main path, cross it and head downhill on stony path opposite. Ignore any turns and follow path as it zig-zags down to a gate. Go through and take grassy track ahead to paved path. Turn L and follow down steps and over footbridge to gravel track and road. Walk through Edale village to start.

0 Distance	Time	Grade
10km/6¼miles	3 hours	Moderate

PLAN YOUR ROUTE

ROUTE

Is it for me? Grassland, woodland, quiet lanes; mostly gentle slopes; but two are quite steep; suitable for most adults, children and dogs
Stiles 10

START/PARKING

Adam's Hill, between Fountain Inn and Hill Tavern, grid ref SO925797
Nearest town Stourbridge
Refreshments Bell and Cross, Holy Cross; Hill Tavern, Fountain Inn and Mount Hotel at Adam's Hill; Vine Inn, Vine Lane; NT café at Nimmings (400m from route
Public toilets Nimmings
Public transport Hanson's Stourbridge-Bromsgrove 318, Mon–Sat; Midland Rider Kidderminster-Hagley circular 197, Mon–Fri

MAPS

Ordnance Survey Explorer 219; Landranger 139

Looking east from Walton Hill towards Romsley – see Point 4.

Photo: Julie Royle

CENTRAL ENGLAND

**Admire panoramic views from the Clent Hills, explore lovely Sling Common and enjoy the tranquillity of St Kenelm's Well.
By Julie Royle.**

❶ Start
Walk past Hill Tavern and bear L on rising path. Climb to a plateau then choose any route to top of Adam's Hill. Join North Worcestershire Path (NWP) and head east to meet a lane. Turn L, ignore two turnings and follow Chapel Lane to St Kenelm's Church. Visit well, return to Chapel Lane, turn L, then R on to Uffmoor Lane. Cross stile next to The Wesleys, go diagonally up field, find a concealed exit to lane, join an unsigned path opposite and climb to Walton Hill summit.

❷ 3km/1¾ miles
Rejoin NWP and follow it south across Walton Hill and Calcot Hill. Approaching Calcot Hill Farm, descend L to Shut Mill Lane. Turn R, then straight on at a junction, leaving NWP. Take L branch when lane forks, then turn L on Woodfield Lane. Turn R on Newtown Lane at a crossroads, then R at T-junction. Pass Bay Tree Cottage then turn R on unsigned path across wooded Sling Common. Keep straight on at junction, turn L past a wetland, then R through more woodland.

❸ 6.5km/4 miles
Rejoining Shut Mill Lane, turn L and then keep straight on along a 'no through road'/bridleway. Pass a house then turn R on another bridleway, soon crossing a cattle grid to join a track to Calcot Hill Farm.

The Four Stones folly on Adam's Hill, near the end of your walk.

Turn L opposite farm entrance, still on bridleway/farm track. When farm track goes L keep straight on along bridleway.

❹ 8km/5 miles
When bridleway turns L go straight ahead on cross-field footpath. Continue through another field to intercept a cross-path, turn R and climb Walton Hill. Pass house and keep climbing to access land. Turn L on bridleway, keeping to L edge of access land and ignoring another bridleway forking R. Go straight on at next junction, joining a footpath, and then turn R on another path. Descend to Vine Lane, turn R then take a bridleway opposite Clatterbach Lane. Climb to a junction and turn L across Adam's Hill back to start.

DORSET
CERNE ABBAS GIANT

Country **walking**

4.5	**Distance** 14.5km/9 miles		**Time** 4½ hours		**Grade** Moderate

PLAN YOUR ROUTE

ROUTE

Is it for me? Chalk downland paths and tracks; 2km stretch of country road
Stiles None
Suitable for older children and dogs

START/PARKING

Car park at Giant View, on A352, just north of Cerne Abbas, grid ref ST663016
Nearest town Dorchester
Refreshments Good choice of pubs in Cerne Abbas; Smiths Arms, Godmanstone (said to be the smallest pub in Britain)
Public toilets Opposite Royal Oak, Cerne Abbas
Public transport Bus D12 runs between Dorchester and Sherborne via Cerne Abbas

MAPS

Ordnance Survey Explorer 117; Landranger 194

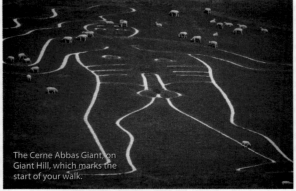

The Cerne Abbas Giant, on Giant Hill, which marks the start of your walk.

Photo: David Noton / Alamy

SOUTHERN ENGLAND

This route, which starts from Dorset's (in)famous hill-figure, explores some of the county's lovely, rolling chalk downland. There are fine views from the ridge tops, and, once away from the Giant, you're unlikely to meet many, if any, other people. The walk goes past the magnificent Minterne Gardens, which are open to the public from the beginning of March to the end of October. By **Fiona Barltrop**

❶ Start
Cerne Abbas is best known for the Cerne Giant whose impressive proportions inevitably provoke comment! Not surprisingly, he has long been seen as a symbol of fertility. Above is an ancient earthwork known as the Trendle or Frying Pan. From Giant View head down road that leads into village, but almost immediately turn off L along lane and across bridge over River Cerne. Follow signs for 'Giant Walk', which will lead you gently up hillside of Giant Hill. Continue along ridge to barn, turn L and go down through gate. Soon turn R and follow bridleway along top of Little Minterne Hill. At gravel lane turn L. This is a fine, broad, ridge-top track, with splendid views over rolling country; to the L Minterne House is prominent in valley below. About 500m along track branch off L and follow bridleway down to Minterne Magna and A352, where you come out by small 15th-century church.

❷ 5km/3 miles
Hidden from road behind high stone walls is Minterne House (not open to the public, but its splendid gardens are). The Minterne Valley was landscaped in manner of Capability Brown in 18th-century when chain of small lakes and cascades was created. Turn L along main road and just after road bends L, turn R and follow path up through an avenue of trees. Continue along bridleway that drops down through trees on other side of hill to Tarmac track.

❸ 6.5km/4 miles
Turn R and soon L to climb up Wether Hill. Go straight across Gore Hill, then bear L along ridge-top track, which is Wessex Ridgeway. Keep along to road. (Note: footpath down through Cerne Park back to car park is not recommended: very muddy in parts!)

❹ 12km/7½ miles
Turn L and follow quiet road down Dickley Hill which will bring you back to main road. Cross straight over and make your way back through village to start. Little remains of once great Benedictine abbey (which gives village second half of its name), but gatehouse, guest-house and impressive 14th-century tithe barn survive.

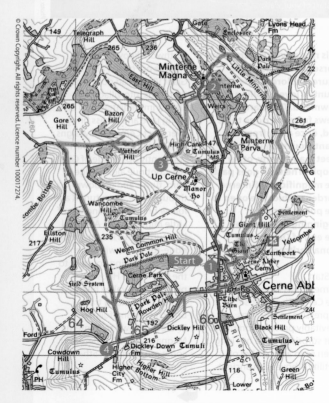

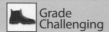
16 Distance
16km/10 miles

Time
5 hours

Grade
Challenging

PLAN YOUR ROUTE

Shaftesbury
Sherborne
kerne Blandford Forum
Ringwood Brockenhu
Wimborne Minster
DORSET New Milton
Dorchester Poole Bournemouth
Wareham
Weymouth Swanage
Fortuneswell
Portland Bill

ROUTE

Is it for me? Downland ridgetop bridleway and Coast Path; number of quite strenuous ascents and descents
Stiles 6
Suitable for older, energetic children and reasonably fit adults

START/PARKING

NT car park north of South Down Farm, above Ringstead Bay, grid ref SY757824 (alternatively large car park at Lulworth Cove, where you would join route midway)
Nearest town Weymouth
Refreshments Lulworth Cove
Public toilets Lulworth Cove
Public transport Not to start, but buses to Lulworth Cove

MAPS

Ordnance Survey Explorer OL15; Landranger 194

The unmistakable spectacle of Durdle Door – see Point 3.

Photo: Fiona Barltrop

SOUTHERN ENGLAND

The Dorset and East Devon coast – known as the Jurassic Coast – is England's first natural World Heritage Site. It covers 95 miles of stunning coastline, with rocks recording 185 million years of Earth's history. One of the most spectacular features is Durdle Door, a dramatic natural archway pierced by the sea. This lies to the west of Lulworth Cove along a superb stretch of chalk cliff coastline. By Fiona Barltrop.

❶ Start
From car park head south-east along broad ridgetop track – fine, easy walking with excellent views along coast in both directions and inland.

❷ 5km/3 miles
Before reaching Dagger's Gate

take footpath which leads R to Newlands Farm, with open access area of notably named Scratchy Bottom below. Turn R and follow road down to Durdle Door Holiday Park caravan site (which can't have failed to catch your attention already; a bit of a scenic eyesore). The footpath goes R through park on eastern edge. At south end head south-east over hill to join Coast Path just west of Lulworth Cove. If you don't want the detour down to Lulworth Cove simply turn R here and set off along Coast Path. Otherwise follow broad stony track down to cove.

❸ 8km/5 miles
Lulworth Cove is picture-postcard-pretty, but pays the price for its popularity. The contorted strata of limestone on either side of cove can be

➡

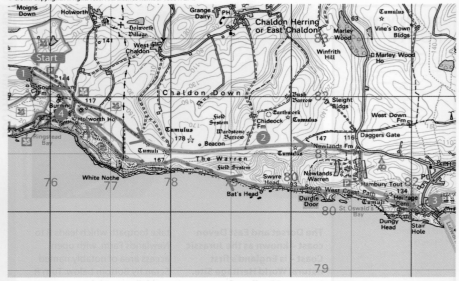

seen (eg at Stair Hole, which is well-signed), and more about the underlying geology of area which is responsible for creating the dramatic coastline can be discovered at the excellent heritage centre. Return leg of this walk follows superb Coast Path westwards, as far as Ringstead Bay, taking in famous Durdle Door and the fine viewpoints of Swyre Head and White Nothe. Stay on Coast Path until you reach driveway to Holworth House.

Swyre Head and beach with Bat's Head beyond.

View over Lulworth Cove, looking from the west.

❹ 14.5km/9 miles
Here leave coast and go R uphill, soon rejoining your outward ridgetop track route. Turn L and car park is 1km away.

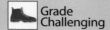
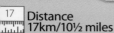
Distance
17km/10½ miles

Time
5 hours

Grade
Challenging

PLAN YOUR ROUTE

ROUTE
Is it for me? Grassy downland, chalk tracks, clifftop paths
Stiles 4
Suitable for older children with stamina; dogs on lead where necessary

START/PARKING
Crown Inn, Shorwell (two car parks for use of patrons), grid ref SZ456830
Nearest town Newport
Refreshments Alum Bay and Freshwater Bay
Public toilets Alum Bay and Fredshwater Bay
Public transport Wightlink Ferries, choice of three routes, tel: 0870 582 7744, www.wightlink.co.uk Hourly Southern Vectis buses between Alum Bay and Shorwell

MAPS
Ordnance Survey Explorer 29; Landranger 196

Evening light over the famous Needles – see Point 4.

Photo: Fiona Bartrop

SOUTHERN ENGLAND

The Isle of Wight has one of the best-maintained footpath and bridleway networks of any county in England. The waymarking is unique: every right of way is allocated a number prefixed by the initial letters of the parish, district or borough through which it passes. There's a long-distance coastal path, as well as eight official trails. This linear route follows one of the finest and most exhilarating of these, the Tennyson Trail, which runs along the crest of the Downs out to the western tip of the island. Bus service back to the start. By Fiona Barltrop.

❶ **Start**
From Crown Inn at Shorwell, turn R and head down road to find a path turn off between two houses on R. Take R-hand

bridleway route which initially heads north before bearing north-west to climb quite steeply up grassy slopes to ridge top. Here turn L along Worsley Trail to Limerstone Down – a fine viewpoint. The downland here provides some of best views on island and on a clear day its whole length and breadth can be seen. Continue north-west along track, which is joined by Tennyson Trail from R – whose route you now follow down to road.

❷ **4km/2½ miles**
On opposite side of road is Mottistone Down car park. On chalk ridge there are a number of round barrows dating back to early Bronze Age – your route climbs steadily up to these barrows and then descends again to B3399.

❸ 6.5km/4 miles
Across road go through a gate
on to NT-owned Brook and
Compton Downs. Track climbs
up past Five Barrows tumuli
and continues along ridge over
Brook and Afton Down
(through a golf course), then
descends to Freshwater Bay.

❹ 11.5km/7 miles
Freshwater Bay is a small bay
with a pebbly beach. Ahead
lies Tennyson Down, a stretch
of fine, open downland,
leading to south-west point of
island and its most famous
landmark, three chalk outcrops
of rock known as the Needles.

Up road a short distance is
Dimbola Lodge, former home
of Julia Margaret Cameron, a
pioneer Victorian
photographer and friend of
Tennyson, who lived nearby at
Farringford House (now a
hotel). Just beyond the
museum is St Agnes Church,
the island's only thatched
church. Tennyson Trail joins
westbound coastal path on
lane to Fort Redoubt, then
ascends grassy slopes of
Tennyson Down whose
summit is marked by a trig
point and memorial to the
poet. Continue on in the
same direction.

❺ 16km/10 miles
As you approach Needles steps
lead down to a spectacular
viewpoint over them from high
above Scratchell's Bay. Beyond
lies the Old Battery, a fort built
in the 1860s. As you follow the
roadside path towards Alum
Bay there are good views of its
famous multi-coloured sand
cliffs. The Alum Bay complex's
man-made 'attractions' come
as quite a shock after the
wonderful, unspoilt scenery up
to now.

 Distance 13.6km/8½ miles	Time 4½ hours	Grade Moderate

PLAN YOUR ROUTE

ROUTE

Is it for me? Long section of open moorland; well-signed permissive path; three long, gentle ascents
Stiles 7
Suitable for All active walkers; dogs on lead on farmland

START/PARKING

Rough Tor car park, grid ref SX138819
Nearest town Camelford
Refreshments None
Public toilets None
Public transport None

MAPS

Ordnance Survey Explorer 109; Landranger 200

View of Rough Tor from the top of Brown Willy – see Point 5.

Photo: Chris Logan

Cornwall may not be famed for its high peaks but the jagged ridge of Brown Willy (420m) and high rock buttresses of the neighbouring Rough Tor (400m) tower majestically above the surrounding moors. Enjoy the panoramic views from these airy heights and the solitude of the open, grass moorland below, but heed the warning signs of the dangers of adders, quaking bogs and rapidly descending mists in this remote area. By Chris Logan.

❶ Start
Cross bridge other side of gate. Start up main path, but at 'Rough Tor National Trust' sign fork R with memorial to Charlotte Dymond, murdered here by her lover in 1844, below you. Follow short grass before swinging R to climb

Louden Hill above reservoir of Stannon China clay works. Enjoy fine views of Rough Tor and ridge of Brown Willy, L, and Garrow Tor behind trees straight ahead.

❷ 2.4km/1½ miles
Continue over hill to stay on top of broad ridge to hit roadway at top of crest. Cross road and stay on highest ground to head across wide spaces of King Arthur's Downs. When you join a grass track that runs level with wall on R follow it to King Arthur's Hall, grassy mounds on skyline, and explore this strange rectangle of stones set round a large reedy hollow.

❸ 5.2km/3¼ miles
Head half-L from stile to small standing stone marking main track. Continue to corner of wall and follow it past gate to Brown Willy Farm before descending to

Left: Climb the Brown Willy ridge – see Point 4.

conifer plantation. Follow path across stream and through narrow strip of trees to marked path between Garrow Tor and little De Lank river. At gateway to ruins of Fernacre Farm enjoy view of Brown Willy before forking R.

❹ 7.6km/4¾ miles
Follow footpath below clump of trees and down to river where bridges and stiles guide you through wet area. After second stile head half-R to pick up path leading between waymarked posts. From top post, where path runs alongside fence, enjoy impressive panoramic spread of four main tors. Descend to cross stream and on other side of track start long but gentle ascent to summit of Brown Willy.

❺ 13.6km/8½ miles
Admire view from highest point in Cornwall, before following grass path down to re-cross De Lank river. Climb track up short slope then head diagonally R up to Showery Tor at end of ridge. From its carefully balanced boulders turn L along ridge of high rocky outcrops with magnificent views northwards to sea. Continue past Little Rough Tor to main tor to inspect Logan stone, then take small path to R from end buttress that leads down over rocks to short grass and head straight across moorland back to car park.

9.5 Distance 9.5km/6 miles	Time 4 hours	Grade Challenging

Walk between the two highest points in southern England.

Photo: Steve Goodier

SOUTHERN ENGLAND

PLAN YOUR ROUTE

- Hartland
- Bideford
- Great Torrington
- South Moltc
- Tiverto
- Holsworthy
- Crediton
- Okehampton
- DEVON
- Exeter
- ceston
- Tavistock
- Liskeard
- Saltash
- Torpoint
- Plymouth
- Plympton
- Ashburton
- Buckfastleigh
- Totnes
- Nev
- Torquay
- Pa
- Da

ROUTE

Is it for me? Mixture of good military roads, moor paths and tracks; some very wild and rough trackless terrain where care must be taken; avoid misty weather
Stiles None
Suitable for experienced walkers adept with map and compass; dogs on lead

START/PARKING

Roadside parking on edge of moor road south of military camp (marked Anthony Stile on map), grid ref
Nearest town Okehampton
Refreshments Cafés and pubs in Okehampton
Public toilets None on route
Public transport None suitable for start

MAPS

Ordnance Survey Explorer OL28; Landranger 191

Dartmoor is quite rightly known as England's last great wilderness – not a place for those who can't navigate and yet on a good day it can be enchanting. It is also home to the two highest points in southern England. Yes Tor (619m) and High Willhays (621m) are in fact higher than anything until you reach Kinder Scout in the Peak District. This moorland route connects the two and uses military roads, moor paths and trackless ground to weave a great circuit over this part of Dartmoor.
By Steve Goodier.

❶ Start
From Anthony Stile pass through green barrier taking upper track L of flag marker poles. There is a small 'No

Unauthorised Vehicles' sign at the start of it. Follow good track rising steadily, ignoring any turnings L or R. As track levels, pass a pond L and after a junction of paths reach a second, bigger junction where track forks.

❷ 1km/½ mile
Go L and descend towards lower slopes of Yes Tor with deep trench of Red-A-Ven Brook ahead, R. Reach ford, cross carefully and leave track to ascend steep trackless ground ahead. A faint grass path develops; follow this, crossing a traversing track. When path vanishes, continue uphill (south) weaving a way carefully through heather and boulders to reach granite tors on summit of Yes Tor. Pass army observation hut, R, and climb to trig point.

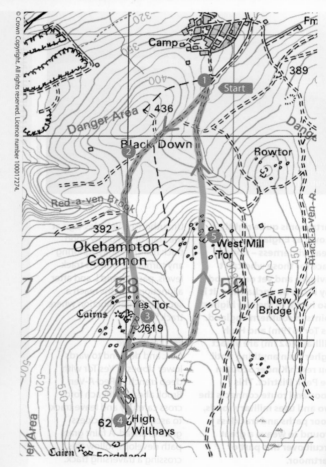

towards R-hand tors of West Mill Tor. Go L at lower tors and walk on good path to rocks of West Mill Tor.

⑤ 7km/4¾ miles
A path goes to L of tor and heads north between lower tors. Track soon vanishes and a way has to be picked downhill through very rough terrain with lots of heather and boulders. You are heading for road in sight below and when ground gets rougher, head R to pick up easier ground and descend to road. Go L, ignoring tracks R and L as you walk back to your car.

NOTE: The Army still use live ammunition on Dartmoor. Most weekends are okay but check before leaving home with Okehampton Tourist Information on 01837 53020 or the High Moorland Visitor Centre on 01822 890414.

Enjoy your walk on Dartmoor – "England's last great wilderness."

❸ 2.9km/1¾ miles
From summit take good track south, descend to col and cross a track. Climb gradually southwards along wide grass track to reach huge cairn on summit of High Willhays.

❹ 4.3km/2¾ miles
Retrace your steps north to col, go R on track and pick up an excellent military road. Follow it bending L, cross ford and when it bends slightly R look for grassy path over moor, L,

SOMERSET
CHEDDAR GORGE

 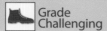

Country **walking**

Distance 10.5km/6½ miles	**Time** 3 hours	**Grade** Challenging

PLAN YOUR ROUTE

ROUTE
Is it for me? Limestone upland; stiff climbs
Stiles 9
Suitable for active walkers and well-controlled dogs

START/PARKING
Riverside Inn, Cheddar, 220m up B3135 from A371, grid ref ST461537
Nearest town Weston-super-Mare
Refreshments Teashops, pubs, cafés in Cheddar
Public toilets Cheddar
Public transport First run regular buses from Weston-super-Mare to Wells

MAPS
Ordnance Survey Explorer 141; Landranger 182

Views from the clifftops at Cheddar Gorge are breathtaking.

Photo: Nigel Vile

SOUTHERN ENGLAND

Cheddar Gorge is one of the most famous natural features in Britain. Carved out of the limestone by rivers that now pass deep underground, what is left is a series of vertical cliffs of up to 450ft in height. The views from the clifftops are truly breathtaking, including an unfenced drop to the road below, where the passing cars look like toys! Beyond the gorge lie a series of nature reserves – Long Wood, Black Rock and Velvet Bottom – a pleasing mixture of deciduous woodland, limestone grassland and a dry river valley where the Romans once extracted lead. A delightful walk with interest and intrigue at every turn. By Nigel Vile.

❶ **Start**
Leave car park, turn R and walk up through Cheddar village for 350m. Turn L along a track that runs in front of Rose Cottage, just a few yards before the Tourist Information Centre, R. In 75m, turn R at a handgate to follow a permissive path steeply uphill for 800m. Beyond a handgate almost on hilltop, walk ahead – bearing slightly R – to follow a path that runs alongside a walk. Continue following this path gently uphill to next gate, before continuing along a hilltop path that drops downhill in 550m to a stepped stile over a wall. Cross and follow a path ahead that bears slightly to R to stile. Beyond stile, follow a woodland path that drops downhill to gravelled track in Black Rock Reserve.

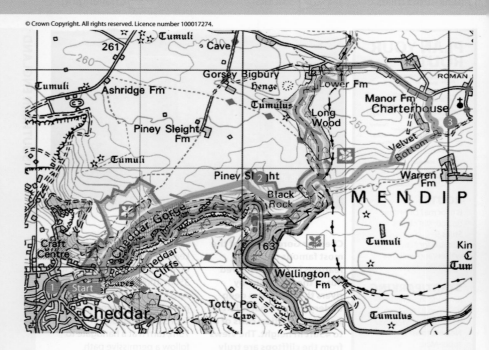

❷ 2.4km/1½ miles
Turn L and follow track for 375m to a gateway. Beyond this, turn R to a gate at entrance to Long Wood. Walk through woodland for 800m, cross footbridge on R and climb uphill to stile at exit from woodland. Follow R edge of field ahead for 100m to stile, turn L and walk across to far R-hand corner of field. Continue along path through scrubland to stile, cross a small paddock to L of a bungalow and continue through woodland – crossing a stream – to join a lane. Turn R and follow a lane

for 800m to driveway leading to Manor Farm. Just past driveway, follow footpath on R across a footbridge and, in another 10m, turn sharp R to a stile on R – potentially muddy spot. Beyond stile, continue along R edge of a field – Manor Farm, R, – for 300m to stile to L of a telegraph pole in end field boundary, keeping L of a clump of nettles at end of field.

❸ 5.2km/3¼ miles
Beyond this stile, continue ahead to outdoor centre and Velvet Bottom. Turn R and follow this dry valley for 1.2km

to a handgate and Black Rock Reserve. Turn L and walk down through Black Rock for 600m to reach B3135. Cross road to stile opposite – slightly to R – and follow a woodland path steeply uphill to gate on hilltop. Beyond gate, follow main well-worn path ahead to another gate before walking across top of Cheddar Gorge for 1.6km to another gate. Continue ahead to a tower, before following a path on L down through trees to a lane. Turn R and, at next junction, turn R and drop downhill to B3135. Turn L back to car park.

Distance	Time	Grade
12.8km/8 miles	4 hours	Moderate

PLAN YOUR ROUTE

Walk through a section of the Avebury Stone Circle at Point 2.

Photo: Nigel Vile

SOUTHERN ENGLAND

ROUTE

Is it for me? Gently undulating chalk downland
Stiles 9
Suitable for fairly active walkers and well-controlled dogs

START/PARKING

National Trust car park, Avebury, grid ref SU098697
Nearest town Swindon
Refreshments Red Lion, Avebury
Public toilets Avebury village centre
Public transport Stagecoach buses run an excellent Trans Wiltshire Express from Swindon to Trowbridge that passes right through Avebury

MAPS

Ordnance Survey Explorer 157; Landranger 173

It is not for nothing that Avebury has been granted World Heritage status. Its earthworks and stone circle are described as Britain's largest megalithic prehistoric monument, whilst nearby Silbury Hill is renowned for being the largest artificial mound in Europe. Close by is West Kennet Long Barrow – England's longest barrow containing a megalithic chamber. By Nigel Vile.

❶ Start
Leave car park, turn R for 20m, turn L through gateway and follow bridleway to handgate. Continue along enclosed path alongside River Kennet for 550m to handgate, before following R edge of field to gate and A4, ignoring R turn across bridge along way. Turn L and, in 20m, pass through handgate, R, to follow path to West Kennet Long Barrow. Beyond river and handgate, follow enclosed path to L to oak tree. A detour R will bring you to barrow – for main walk keep ahead along bottom L edge of field to gate and stile, before continuing along short section of track to lane.

❷ 2.4km/1½ miles
Cross lane to stile, and follow R edge of field to stile in far R corner. Continue along enclosed path to its junction with track, turn L and walk down to lane. Turn L, cross Kennet before turning R along bridleway. Follow path along bottom edge of field to track, turn L and walk up to A4. Follow Ridgeway opposite for 800m to junction. Turn L, walk across to a clump of beech trees and keep on path as it bears R. In 800m, turn L – NT

waymark on post – and follow
R edges of two fields down to
B4003. Cross to handgate
opposite, turn R and follow
path along through avenue. At
far end of this line of stones,
pass through handgate, cross
to gateway opposite, turn L
and walk down through a
section of the Avebury Stone
Circle to a gate and Red Lion.

❸ 6.4km/4 miles
Turn L and, where main road
bears L, keep ahead along
Avebury's High Street. In 180m,
turn R into churchyard and
bear half-L to gate in L-hand
wall. Walk along enclosed path
– it becomes a back lane – to

pumping station. Continue
along Tarmac path, cross
Kennet and keep R at fork. Path
soon becomes lane – keep
ahead for 225m to junction.
Follow road to R for 225m to
junction by barn. Keep ahead
for 1.6km to T-junction with
track, turn R and continue for
400m to junction. Keep ahead
and follow track for 800m on to
Windmill Hill. Having emerged
from woodland on hilltop,
keep ahead for a few paces
before passing through a
handgate on R.

❹ 10.4km/6½ miles
Climb to summit of Windmill
Hill, and walk across hilltop to

most distant round barrow.
Pass through gateway beyond
barrow, and follow L edges of
two fields downhill. Just
beyond second field, cross stile
on R and walk length of field to
series of stiles in end field
boundary. Follow L edge of
next field to stile and, in
following field, walk ahead to
stile in opposite boundary.
Cross next field to footbridge
in opposite field boundary,
before turning L down to stile
and footpath. Turn L and
retrace steps back into centre
of Avebury where L turn is
signposted back to NT car park.

WEST SUSSEX
DEVIL'S DYKE

Country **walking**

Distance
12km/7¼miles

Time
3½ hours

Grade
Moderate

PLAN YOUR ROUTE

The spectacular Devil's Dyke was cut by glacial meltwaters.

Photo: David Hancock

ROUTE
Is it for me? Rolling chalk downland, field paths, Tarmac lane; one long and gradual climb; one steep descent and ascent
Stiles 8
Suitable for all

START/PARKING
National Trust Summer Down car park, Devil's Dyke Estate, grid ref TQ269111
Nearest town Brighton
Refreshments Royal Oak, Poynings; Shepherd & Dog, Fulking; Devil's Dyke pub
Public toilets At main Devil's Dyke car park
Public transport Bus 77 from Brighton Pier, weekends and Bank Holidays, daily in July and August

MAPS
Ordnance Survey Explorer 122; Landranger 198

This glorious walk of contrasts begins by climbing the flanks and then descends through the Devil's Dyke, a spectacular, steep-sided downland combe or cleft 91m deep and 800m long, which was cut by glacial meltwaters during the Ice Age. Head across fields to the pretty village of Fulking and the perfectly positioned Shepherd & Dog pub, both tucked away at the foot of the Downs, before a steep haul leads you back to the top of the South Downs escarpment and the South Downs Way. You then walk to the motte and bailey earthwork at the top of Edburton Hill for stunning views across the Weald and south across rolling downland landscape to Brighton and the sea, before heading back along the

South Downs Way back to the Devil's Dyke Estate (NT). By David Hancock.

❶ Start
From car park go through gate and bear R along South Downs Way (SDW), passing reservoir before descending steeply to gate and road. Bear L for few paces, then turn L through gate. Bear slightly L and follow defined path across field to stile. With Devil's Dyke ahead, keep ahead and soon merge with wide path. Head uphill and keep R at junctions above valley to reach head of dry valley. Take path that steeply descends down the valley, bearing L at fork at bottom to climb stile.

❷ 3.2km/2 miles
Ascend steps into woodland, path soon levelling and curving L through trees to

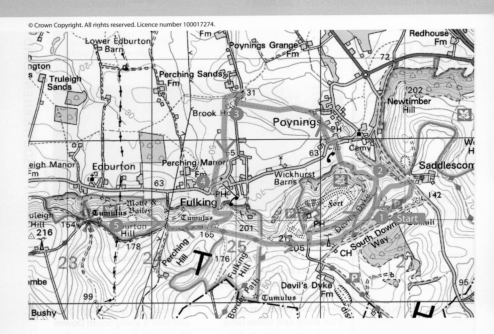

bridleway. Turn R down sunken path and R again at junction by garden. Follow path into Poynings. Turn L along road, then R at bend along brick drive and go through gate. Head across field and bear L at track to cross stream. Climb stile on L, follow track to stile and head straight across field to stile and lane.

❸ 5.2km/3¼ miles
Turn R and soon take footpath L along drive to Brookside. Bear immediately L, following grassy path to junction and turn L over footbridge. Bear L and

soon follow marked path along R-hand edge of fields, heading towards Downs. Cross track via stiles and continue towards Fulking, crossing stile on to grassy path. Turn R, then L in few paces to cross centre of field to kissing-gate. Keep L to kissing-gate and village lane.

❹ 6.6km/4¼ miles
Turn R to Shepherd & Dog pub. Go through car park to join narrow, fenced path beside garden. Cross stile and steeply climb Fulking escarpment to crossing of paths. Turn sharp R and follow sunken path to join

SDW at top of South Downs. Turn R and keep to chalk track down to crossing of paths. Just beyond fence take narrow defined path diagonally R uphill to stile to reach motte and bailey for wonderful all-round views.

❺ 8.4km/5¼ miles
Retrace steps back along SDW and keep to this track to gate. Unless you want to visit Devil's Dyke pub, ignore path that sweeps L and keep ahead, following SDW to road. Go through gate opposite and follow SDW back through trees to car park.

9.7
Distance
9.7km/6miles

Time
4 hours

Grade
Easy

SOUTHERN ENGLAND

PLAN YOUR ROUTE

ROUTE

Is it for me? Terrain Concrete and Tarmac. Note: Thames Path is signed throughout the walk. However, due to ongoing development of Docklands and Greenwich, the path may be diverted or re-routed. Check www.nationaltrail.co.uk/ThamesPath for details
Stiles None
Suitable for all

START/PARKING

Plaza at Canary Wharf, grid ref TQ374802; few parking options
Nearest town London!
Refreshments Various pubs, cafés, tearooms and coffee bars
Public toilets Canary Wharf Shopping Centre
Public transport Docklands Light Railway and Jubilee Line Underground both stop at Canary Wharf; nearest overground station for return journey is Charlton

MAPS

Ordnance Survey Explorer 162; Landranger 177

Your walk starts amidst the skyscrapers at Canary Wharf.

Photo: Jamie Smith

Walk the final miles of the Thames Path – Canary Wharf to the Thames Barrier – and discover why urban exploration can sometimes offer as much reward as country walking. You'll pass some of the most famous sights in Britain, old and new – One Canada Square, the Cutty Sark basin, the Royal Naval College, Greenwich Observatory, The O2 (once the Millennium Dome) and the Thames Barrier, and encounter a strange landscape of docks, jetties and art installations. Your feet will ache (concrete hurts!), but the experience will be unforgettable. By Nick Hallissey.

❶ Start
Standing in main plaza with Jubilee Line station L, walk south and cross bridge over dock. Turn R and follow road to busy road junction with A1206 (Westferry Road). Turn L and carefully cross A1206, reaching access lock on far side. Walk past lock and turn R, signed 'Thames Path' and proceed to Thames riverbank, where a fine view into Central London unfolds. Turn L and follow 'Thames Path' signs south on western side of Isle of Dogs. Path occasionally swings inland to avoid residential areas, but signs are consistent. At southern tip of Isle, path passes Napier Avenue and the remains of the SS Great Eastern's launch ramp, before proceeding to the brick-and-glass dome marking the entrance to the Greenwich Foot Tunnel.

❷ 3.3km/2 miles
Enter tunnel, descending via stairs or lift, and cross to

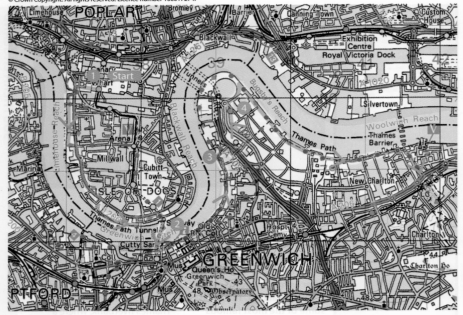

Greenwich side, emerging at Cutty Sark dry dock. Thames Path turns L directly, but a detour may be made into Greenwich itself, plus attractions such as National Maritime Museum and Royal Greenwich Observatory, by proceeding due south past Cutty Sark. Regaining Thames Path, pass Royal Naval College and continue on south bank through residential areas, passing Trafalgar Tavern and The Yacht, two pubs with river frontage. Path continues along industrial wharves, veering

north on Greenwich peninsula, until it turns sharp R to head inland towards A102.

❸ 5.5km/3½ miles
Path proceeds through several alleys to reach footbridge across A102 (Blackwall Tunnel Approach). On far side, head north, following signs for Thames Path, The O2 and North Greenwich Tube Station. Skirt tube station to reach entrance to The O2. Entry to cafés and restaurants is free.

❹ 7.1km/4½ miles
Leave The O2 to re-emerge on riverbank on east side of peninsula, passing a series of scattered art installations and, further south, the David Beckham Football Academy. Follow clear Thames Path waymarks, passing industrial jetties, loading docks and a large Sainsburys distribution centre, before reaching Thames Barrier – end of Thames Path. Turn R and follow industrial estate road south to meet A206 (Woolwich Road). Turn R and follow road for about 1km to Charlton Station.

GLOUCESTERSHIRE
PAINSWICK

Country walking

![clock] Distance	![time] Time	![boot] Grade
16km/10miles	5 hours	Moderate

16

PLAN YOUR ROUTE

Woodland near Dillay Brook and Snow's Hill – see Point 3.

Photo: Julie Royle

SOUTHERN ENGLAND

ROUTE
Is it for me? Woodland and pasture, moderately hilly, steep in places
Stiles 13
Suitable for most adults, children and dogs

START/PARKING
Painswick High Street, grid ref SO865095
Nearest town Stroud
Refreshments Painswick
Public toilets Painswick
Public transport Stagecoach 46, daily from Stroud and Cheltenham

MAPS
Ordnance Survey Explorer 179; Landranger 162 & 163

The hills and valleys round Painswick form possibly the loveliest part of the Cotswolds, and are blessed with numerous footpaths, as well as commons and nature reserves with Open Access, several of which feature in this walk. By Julie Royle.

❶ **Start**
Go diagonally across churchyard, continue to The Cross, then descend Tibbiwell Lane. Cross Painswick Stream and turn L, following it to lane. Turn R uphill, then R on another lane. Turn L at T-junction, fork R after Field House then enter woodland. Go uphill to meet bridleway and turn L. Keep straight on into Blackstable Wood. Shortly fork R, away from woodland edge. Reaching five-ways junction, take middle path of three ahead. Keep straight on

at four more junctions but descend L soon after passing stile. Turn R along lane and straight on at a junction.

❷ 4km/2½ miles
Turn R on footpath, climb to road and continue opposite, across field to lane. Turn L. Take first footpath on R, walking through field and copse then turning R on track. Descend through woodland to junction. Turn R, shortly entering field. Follow track to gate then keep R of Dillay Brook down valley. Pass through gateway to join track along valley side. Keep straight on at junction.

❸ 6.5km/4 miles
Drawing level with house, descend L to bridge then diagonally R uphill to wood. Turn R, pass L of cottage then cross track, going straight on along path. Turn R at cross-

➡

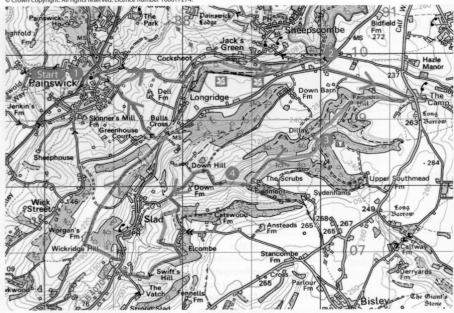

Enjoy the meadow flowers and
grasses on this Gloucestershire walk.

path, follow Dillay Brook
through woodland, meadow,
then more woodland to
another meadow. Take path
high on valley side before
descending diagonally to
bottom corner of Snow's Farm
Nature Reserve.

❹ 8km/5 miles
Go through gate, turn R, climb
to Snow's Farm and turn L. Turn
L again at road junction, then L
on byway after Steanbridge
Mill. Climb to cross-path. Turn R
through woodland, fork L and

enter field. Keep straight on.
Path becomes a track, bending
L at Furners Farm to meet a
lane. Turn R, and R again at a
junction. Take path after The
Vatch Cottage. Climb to road,
turn R, then take first path on L.
Climb Wickridge Hill then turn
R along track. Keep straight on
to Frith Wood, walk to far end,
turn L on a track and straight
on at a junction, along
Greenhouse Lane to Painswick.

CORNWALL
PORT ISAAC–ROCK

19/14.5 Distance 19km/12miles or 14.5km/9 miles	Time 4/6 hours	Grade Challenging

PLAN YOUR ROUTE

Bude
Boscastle • Tintagel • Launceston •
Padstow • Wadebridge Tav
Bodmin •
• Liske
wquay • CORNWALL Salta
St Austell Torp
se • Looe
• Truro Fowey
• Redruth

ROUTE

Is it for me? Well-signed coast path (South West Coast Path), first part to Port Quin the most strenuous
Stiles 6
Suitable for walkers with stamina; Polzeath to Rock section recommended for families with young children

START/PARKING

Park at Polzeath or Rock and take bus to Port Isaac for start of walk, grid ref SW998809
Nearest town Wadebridge
Refreshments ort Isaac, Polzeath and Rock
Public toilets Port Isaac, Polzeath and Rock
Public transport Western Greyhound 584 bus service between Rock and Port Isaac, via Polzeath, daily every two hours (except winter Sundays)

MAPS

Ordnance Survey Explorer 106; Landranger 200

The coastline west of Port Isaac, between Points 1 and 2.

Photo: Fiona Barltrop

SOUTHERN ENGLAND

Those who've watched ITV's 'Doc Martin' (with Martin Clunes) will be very familiar with the fishing village of Port Isaac on the North Cornwall coast, even if they've never been there! It's a picturesque place indeed, so hardly surprising it was chosen as the location for the filming of the series. Between here and Polzeath is a most delightful and highly scenic stretch of the South West Coast Path, much of it in the care of the National Trust, including the wonderful Rumps and Pentire points. There's a good bus service linking Port Isaac with Polzeath and Rock, so a linear walk is no problem. By Fiona Barltrop.

❶ **Start**
Polzeath has a large beach car park, which fills up quickly in

summer and on sunny weekends, since this is a favourite surfers' beach. Indeed, it's probably best avoided at these times! Alternatively, New Polzeath, Daymer Bay and Rock also have car parks. If you decide to park at Rock car park (near ferry landing) it's a 1.5km walk up road to bus stop (at Rock Clock Garage). Take bus from Polzeath (or Rock) to Port Isaac where you'll be dropped off at top of village. Walk down to harbour and continue up lane on its west side which leads to Coast Path proper. Now just follow National Trail acorn symbols keeping sea on your R! First 4.8km to Port Quin take you round Varley and Kellan heads, involving quite a lot of up and down. A super stretch of coast.

❷ 4.8km/3 miles
The beautiful Port Quin inlet was once a busy little pilchard port, but it's peaceful today with just a few cottages. Note drinking water tap on wall in front of you as you descend steps to harbour. Carry on up road other side. Look out for a stile, R, which gets you back on to cliffs – lower and more gentle than preceding section. This is National Trust property. On Doyden Point is a little 19th-century folly castle (apparently once used for drinking and gambling parties!), now a National Trust holiday let. Mine shafts west of here were for antimony – a yellow pigment used, among other things, for ceramic glazing. Between Trevan and Carnweather points are Epphaven Cove and Lundy Bay. (Look out for Lundy Hole – a few metres from the path on your R.) Rumps Point – which, together with The Mouls island, has been visible for much of the way – is a marvellous spot, especially for bird-watching. The earth ramparts of an Iron Age fort can be clearly seen.

❸ 12km/7½ miles
Pentire Point is next headland beyond Rumps Point, and a very fine viewpoint.

❹ 14.5km/9 miles
Fom Polzeath, if you want to continue, it's easy walking alongside Camel estuary to Rock. On the way you can make a short detour to St Enodoc's Church, where former poet laureate Sir John Betjeman is laid to rest.

Distance
16km/10miles or 13km/8 miles

Time
5/4 hours

Grade
Challenging

PLAN YOUR ROUTE

ROUTE
Is it for me? Terrain
Grassy downland ridges;
stretch of South West
Coast Path; Swanage
seafront/beach
Stiles 4
Suitable for all (dogs
travel free on Swanage
Railway)

START/PARKING
Car park at Corfe Castle,
grid ref SY958817
Nearest town Swanage
and Wareham
Refreshments Lots of
choice in Corfe Castle
and Swanage
Public toilets None
Public transport
Swanage Railway trains
run every weekend and
Bank Holiday from mid-
February and every day
of the week from April to
October. Regular year-
round daily buses
(service 142/143)
between Swanage and
Poole via Wareham and
Corfe Castle

MAPS
Ordnance Survey
Explorer OL15;
Landranger 395

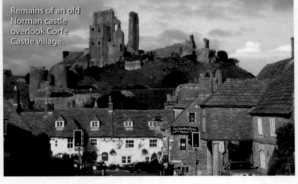

Remains of an old
Norman castle
overlook Corfe
Castle village.

Photo: Fiona Barltrop

SOUTHERN ENGLAND

**Purbeck is one of the
loveliest areas in southern
England, affording
delightful walking with
magnificent views both
along its superb coastline –
part of the Jurassic Coast –
and over the inland Purbeck
Hills, which form an east-
west ridge. To the north of
the ridge low-lying
heathland criss-crossed by
paths provides easier, but
very pleasant walking. This
walk follows a fine stretch of
the Purbeck ridge from Corfe
Castle to the coast – with a
detour to view the famous
Old Harry rocks – and
continues along the coast
path to finish at Swanage. A
ride on the popular Swanage
(steam) Railway –
particularly recommended
for those with children –
returns you to back to the
start. By Fiona Barltrop.**

❶ **Start**
From car park head back into
village centre, go L along main
road and very soon turn R
along Sandy Lane which goes
under railway. Immediately
turn L over stile on to
permissive path signed for 'East
Hill'. It's a steep climb up lots of
steps on to ridge, but once on
top going is much easier. Below
you may hear and see Swanage
Railway steam train as it chuffs
its way up and down valley.
Path links up with bridleway
near Rollington Hill. Head along
ridge-top bridleway towards
mast and continue over
Branscombe Hill and past
several tumuli to trig point on
Nine Barrow Down.

❷ **5.5km/3½ miles**
From Nine Barrow Down
follow track downhill, taking R
fork for Ulwell and just before
road, turn L for Studland Road.

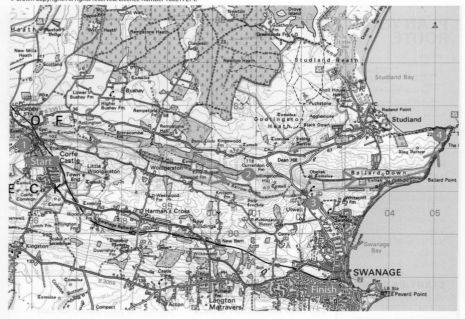

❸ 7km/4¼ miles

At road go R down to second lay-by with information panels and 'Welcome to Swanage' sign. Take footpath on L and go ahead to climb steeply uphill to obelisk. Turn R and follow path westwards along ridge over Ballard Down. For shorter walk you can omit Old Harry rocks and turn R along Coast Path before reaching trig point. Otherwise carry on past Ballard Point until you have a view of Old Harry chalk stacks.

❹ 11km/7 miles

Retrace steps to Ballard Point and continue along Coast Path which leads you into Swanage, a popular family-friendly beach resort. Turn R after passing TIC to head up to railway station and bus stops. Swanage Railway is a six-mile long heritage railway between Swanage and Norden (with a stop at Corfe Castle). Special events are held throughout the year (eg half-term Thomas the Tank Engine weeks). From Corfe Castle stop

it's just a short walk back to car park. (An alternative to train is bus, which also links Swanage with Corfe and runs regularly every day.)

0.5 Distance
20.5km/12¼miles

Time
6 hours

Grade
Challenging

The quaint St Andrew's Church at Jevington – see Point 3.

Photo: Fiona Barltrop

SOUTHERN ENGLAND

PLAN YOUR ROUTE

ROUTE
Is it for me? Downland, cliffs and riverbank path (option of short stretch of forest, too)
Stiles 7 (9 if you take SDW from Exceat to Litlington)
Suitable for appropriately fit walkers

START/PARKING
Car parks in Alfriston, grid ref TQ522034
Nearest town Seaford
Refreshments Tearooms and pubs, Alfriston; pub and tearoom, Jevington; pub, Exceat Bridge; tearoom, Exceat
Public toilets Alfriston and Exceat (visitor centre)
Public transport Mainline trains to Eastbourne via Berwick (bus connection to Alfriston) or Seaford (and bus connection); other bus services, too

MAPS
Ordnance Survey Explorer 123; Landranger 199

Between Alfriston and Eastbourne – where the South Downs Way finishes – there are two routes, an inland bridleway that goes via Jevington, and a footpath that takes you down the Cuckmere Valley to the coast and along the Seven Sisters to Beachy Head. A splendid but long walk can be enjoyed by following the former to Beachy Head and returning along by the latter. By Fiona Barltrop.

❶ Start
From car park head into village centre and turn L along Tarmac path beside United Reformed Church. This leads to open grassy area called the Tye, across which stands the imposing church, known as the 'Cathedral of the Downs'. Beside church is Old Clergy

House, a medieval thatched building and first property purchased by National Trust in 1896 – for £10! Cross footbridge over river and continue ahead to road, turning R along footpath just before it. Follow this for short distance then cross stile to continue along road to T-junction. Go R and soon L on to bridleway.

❷ 1km/½ mile
Follow track which climbs steadily. Another track comes in from R and thereafter you'll reach crossing track near Winchester's Pond. Do pause to look back at views across Cuckmere Valley! Keep ahead, passing Lullington Heath National Nature Reserve, R. Track descends then re-ascends to join up with South Downs Way (SDW). Follow this down to Jevington, passing

lovely flintstone church along the way.

❸ 4.8km/3 miles
At road turn R then almost immediately L by Jevington Tea Rooms, continuing along SDW which ascends Bourne Hill. At top you'll reach a junction of tracks where you turn R.

❹ 6.3km/4 miles
Head south along Willingdon Hill – extensive views – bearing R in front of copse of trees, then L again to continue in same direction which leads to Tarmac lane lined with large houses. This in turn leads to Jevington Road. Turn L up to main road (A259). Cross and go ahead to NT Crowlink car park.

❺ 10.3km/6½ miles
Head south-west to Flagstaff Brow (lane to R leads down to Crowlink village) to reach cliff edge and sarsen stone monument. Here you're about midway along Seven Sisters with wonderful views.

❻ 11.8km/7¼ miles
Turn R and follow cliffs to end – Haven Brow, which overlooks Cuckmere Haven and meanders of Cuckmere Valley. Bear R inland gradually descending to meet valley floor. Opposite turning to Foxhole (a camping barn and campsite) cross to the river bank path and continue to Exceat Bridge.

❼ 15.5km/9¾ miles
Cross road and follow east bank of Cuckmere back to Alfriston. (Alternatively, you could take SDW from Exceat, through edge of Friston Forest, to Litlington, and join riverbank path there.)

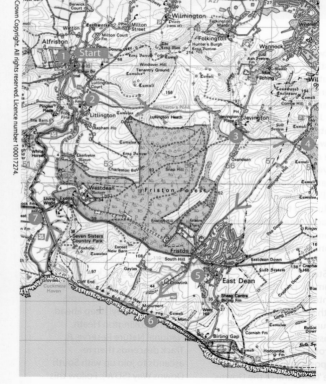

5.4	Distance 15.4km/9½miles	Time 4½ hours	Grade Moderate

On the way down from Leith Hill, soon after Point 5.

Photo: Tom Bailey

SOUTHERN ENGLAND

PLAN YOUR ROUTE

ROUTE
Is it for me? Woodland paths, small section of road, two long uphills. Navigation in woods can be confusing. Suitable for all
Stiles 10+

START/PARKING
Roadside parking at Holmwood Station, grid ref TQ174437
Nearest town Dorking
Refreshments Pubs at Coldharbour and Friday Street; cake and hot drinks available at Leith Hill Tower at weekends
Public toilets None
Public transport Trains from London and Horsham; Arriva bus 93 Dorking-Horsham stops at Holmwood. No buses or trains on Sundays

MAPS
Ordnance Survey Explorer 146; Landranger 187

Head to the roof of Surrey at Leith Hill – the highest point in the county – for views from the capital to the sea. By Jenny Walters.

❶ Start
From station, turn L (north-west) and turn L on footpath at end of houses. Follow between hedges to road, head L and continue to three-way junction. Go straight on, past Moorhurst and into woods. After short distance, turn R over stile and up R-hand side of field to corner. Bear L across next field to corner of woodland and over stile into woods. Follow path uphill, bearing L, over stile, and diagonally R uphill over field towards buildings. Cross stile near farm, turn L to join track through farmyard and follow up to road. Turn R to junction, then L to Coldharbour and pub!

❷ 2.6km/1½ miles
Turn R opposite pub, taking L-hand byway uphill to Coldharbour Cricket Ground. Fork L on track, ignoring green path to far L, and follow byway through woods (marked by wooden posts). Ignore all other minor paths, until you reach a large track junction with signs to tower. Follow waymarked route downhill to R to junction, then L uphill to tower.

❸ 4.3km/2¾ miles
From tower head west, following clear path signed to 'Starveall Corner' car park. Just before car park (you should be able to see it) turn R on bridleway. Walk to path crossroads, turn L and follow to road junction. Cross minor road and join busier road for 50m, then turn R on bridleway,

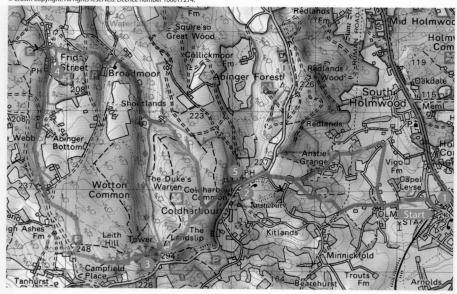

cross another road and follow track straight on into woods beside fence. Continue straight over path crossroads and on to road. Turn L on road, then R on bridleway (ignoring footpath to R) and follow through woods with stream on R, to join road with pub on R.

❹ 7.8km/4¾ miles
Continue up road to junction, turn R and cross pond, then R on path heading uphill through woods to road. Cross over to a second road, cross, and continue on path opposite. At fork, bear R downhill, then L at next junction to road. Turn L on

road, then R on bridleway, following 'Greensand Way' round to R. Ignore paths to L and R, and continue to junction. Fork L signed 'Tilling Springs', ignore path to L, past houses, and turn R on to bridleway at bend. Head uphill, ignoring track to R, to track across path. Turn L then immediately R, to continue uphill. Go straight over crossroads back to cricket ground. Bear L round pitch and back down track to road and pub from earlier!

❺ 11.9km/7½ miles
Turn L on road back to junction, then R, and L on track

back to Anstiebury Farm. Go through farmyard, and continue straight on downhill between fences to buildings (ignoring stile to R you came over earlier). Bear L over stile and follow path over series of stiles to road. Cross road and take path opposite, following R-hand hedge on across a series of fields and on to a track. Follow downhill past buildings to road junction. Turn L to path on corner from earlier and turn R to road, and R again back to station.

HAMPSHIRE
FROGHAM–NEW FOREST

Distance	Time	Grade
13.6km/8½miles	4 hours	Moderate

PLAN YOUR ROUTE

ROUTE
Is it for me? Woodland tracks and paths, some gentle climbs. Suitable for all
Stiles None

START/PARKING
Abbots Well parking near Frogham, grid ref SU177128
Nearest town Fordingbridge
Refreshments Royal Oak, Fritham
Public toilets None
Public transport Very limited bus service from Fordingbridge to Frogham

MAPS
Ordnance Survey Explorer OL22; Landranger 195

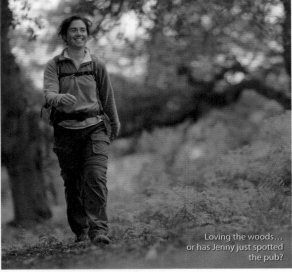

Loving the woods…
or has Jenny just spotted the pub?

Photo: Tom Bailey

SOUTHERN ENGLAND

Explore the quiet western side of the New Forest with this walk around the Fritham Plain. It combines far-reaching views from the Hampton Ridge over heath and trees, with close-up sections through wooded enclosures and beside streams. The Royal Oak in Fritham makes a good lunch spot to catch up on local happenings. By Jenny Walters.

❶ **Start**
From car park, walk to road and turn R downhill to corner. As road swings L, take broad track straight on labelled 'Cycle

Route to Fritham Only'. Head uphill – ignore path coming in from R – to fork in path. Take R-hand option and follow cycleway signs on to Hampton Ridge. At next fork keep L to continue on main track along ridgeline, then R at next fork, and on to path junction. Go straight over on broad track which curves R to edge of woods.

❷ **3.4km/2 miles**
Walk downhill on track through woods, and follow as it swings L at bottom. Keep following as it then swings R (ignore path to L), then L (ignore path to R), and

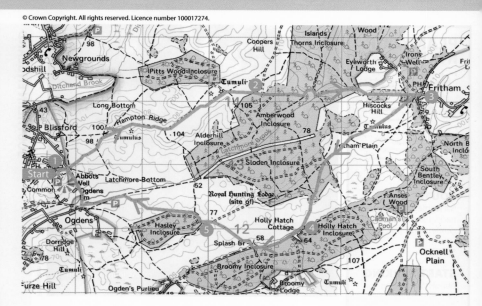

continue to edge of woods. Ignore path from L and bear R on main track gently uphill to edge of Fritham village – head straight on for Royal Oak.

❸ 6.1km/3¾ miles
From pub, head back towards path you walked in on, but soon turn L through car park to take broad track south-west across Hiscocks Hill and Fritham Plain, ignoring all minor paths to L and R. At major track fork just before woods of Sloden Inclosure, bear L to head downhill

through trees. Keep on track to far edge of woods, then on downhill to footbridge.

❹ 9km/5½ miles
Cross bridge and turn R on track in front of white house (Holly Hatch Cottage). As track bends to L, continue straight on along a grassy – and sometimes faint – path along edge of trees. When you reach a gravel track, turn R and cross Splash Bridge, then walk uphill on path bending L, to another track. Turn L on track and walk to edge of Hasley Hill woods.

❺ 10.8km/6¾ miles
Turn R and follow sandy track as it curves round edge of wood to a fork halfway along northern edge. Turn R and go diagonally downhill to Latchmore Brook, then L on faint path parallel to stream, to car park. Turn R through car park and follow track over footbridge beside ford, and on uphill. Continue past farm on L, ignoring all other paths, until you reach road. Turn L up hill and L back to car.

Distance
18km/11miles

Time
6 hours

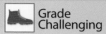
Grade
Challenging

PLAN YOUR ROUTE

ROUTE
Is it for me? Well-marked South West Coast Path – rugged cliffs and river estuary; fields, quiet country lanes. Suitable for fit walkers. Beware cliff edges with dogs and young children
Stiles 5

START/PARKING
North Sands car park at south end of Salcombe town, grid ref SX731383
Nearest town Salcombe
Refreshments North Sands, South Sands, Bolberry Down, Hope Cove
Public toilets South Sands, Hope Cove
Public transport Salcombe is well served by buses. Also passenger ferry from Salcombe to South Sands (Easter to Oct)

MAPS
Ordnance Survey Explorer OL20; Landranger 202

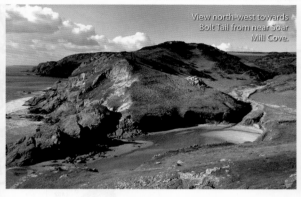
View north-west towards Bolt Tail from near Soar Mill Cove.

Photo: Fiona Barltrop

SOUTHERN ENGLAND

Not only does the South Hams area of South Devon boast some very fine stretches of coastline, several attractive estuaries and a chunk of Dartmoor, but it's also one of the most environmentally friendly, green-minded places in the country, with the highest concentration of GTBS (Green Tourism Business Awards Scheme) award-winning businesses in the South West. Use of public transport is actively encouraged and this walk is an excellent one to do if you'd prefer to manage without the car, but there's plenty of parking for those with cars. The walk follows a superb section of the South West Coast Path from Salcombe to Hope Cove with a pleasant inland return. The

cliff scenery is dramatic, so allow time to enjoy the magnificent views. By Fiona Barltrop.

❶ Start
The first half of this walk is along route of South West Coast Path, so as long as you keep sea on your L and stick to National Trail acorn symbols you shouldn't go wrong! The Salcombe estuary is always full of interest – from North Sands can be seen the remains of a 16th-century artillery fort built by Henry VIII to guard the harbour entrance. From North Sands car park turn R and follow road to South Sands. Soon after Coast Path becomes a proper path as you continue through woodland, then emerge to round Sharp Tor – a fine viewpoint. Starehole Bay lies ahead of you. Descend to

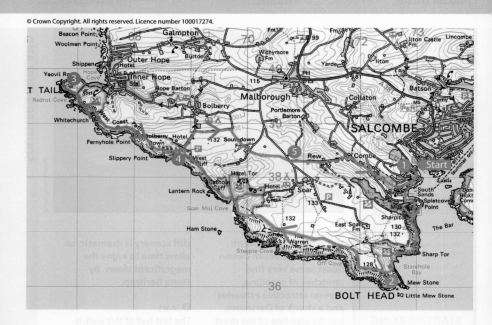

cross a stream and ascend to Bolt Head.

❷ 2.5km/1½ miles
The cliffs between Bolt Head and Bolt Tail are particularly rugged, affording many fine and dramatic views. Not quite midway is attractive Soar Mill Cove – there's quite a descent and corresponding ascent either side. (For a short walk, you can turn inland here towards Soar and join last leg of the main route's return at Rew.) Bolt Tail is site of an Iron Age promontory fort (visible remains). From here you drop down to Hope Cove – though if

not in need of refreshments you could always turn round here, since you have to retrace your steps anyway from Bolt Tail back to Bolberry Down.

❸ 10km/6¼ miles
Hope Cove is an attractive and popular village with a choice of places for refreshment. As mentioned above, return to Bolberry Down car park. (There's a short-cut back to Coast Path if you'd prefer to omit Bolt Tail on your return – which you could also omit altogether, turning in at Bolberry Down on the outward leg.)

❹ 13km/8 miles
At car park head inland past masts and take first path you come to on your R – Jacobs Lane, a restored green lane. Take next R signed for 'South Down Farm'. Cross farm drive then drive to cottages and continue east along a footpath to road.

❺ 15.5km/9¾ miles
Take L fork to Combe via Rew. R at Combe then footpath on L through trees back to South Sands/North Sands.

11.8 Distance
11.8km/7¼miles

Time
4 hours

Grade
Moderate

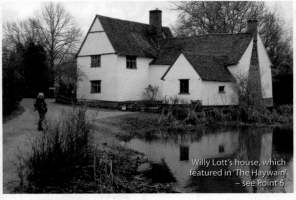

SOUTHERN ENGLAND

Willy Lott's house, which featured in 'The Haywain' – see Point 6.

Photo: Len Banister

PLAN YOUR ROUTE

ROUTE
Is it for me? Mainly easy walking on the Essex Way and the St Edmund Way. Ascents and descents are gradual; can be muddy
Stiles 16

START/PARKING
Large pay-and-display car park at Manningtree Station, grid ref TM094322
Nearest town Ipswich, Colchester
Refreshments Good pubs in Dedham, but for an unusual experience, try Manningtree's Station Buffet with good food and an excellent range of real ales
Public toilets At station; Dedham; Flatford Mill
Public transport Trains from London Liverpool Street via Billericay and Ipswich

MAPS
Ordnance Survey Explorer 196; Landranger 169

The outward and return routes of this glorious walk are contrasted. The walk to Dedham, with its church made famous by Constable, is over almost manicured hilly ground whilst the return along the banks of the River Stour is flat and virtually wild and desolate in places. For many, the visit to Flatford Mill and Willy Lott's House, which feature in 'The Haywain', will be the highlight but this will not diminish the attractions of Dedham or the delight of visiting the Station Buffet at Manningtree. By Len Banister.

❶ Start
Walk between upper and lower car parks to cross R over bridge then L up fenced path to enter churchyard. Leave by car park.

❷ 0.9km/½ mile
You will now be guided by poppy symbols along Essex Way to Dedham. Follow fingerpost diagonally R through gate across field then L on drive to road. Go R then L at drive to Sherbourne, keeping forward through metal gate, along grassy path then L edge of field to go L on to drive. At junction with transformer on pole, fork R. Fork R again then just past pond go R, leaving drive. Follow waymarkers to cross stream and series of stiles over railway.

❸ 2.8km/1¾ miles
Keep forward up field. Three kissing-gates take you to road. Cross slightly R along brow of hill to rejoin road. Go R. At sharp R-hand bend go L along L edge of three fields and along fenced path of two more to drive, then road.

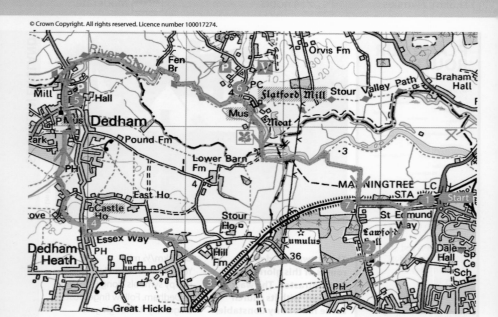

❹ 4.4km/2¾ miles
Go R, soon L at fingerpost.
Cross field, down steps over
stile and along bottom of
wood to cross front of house to
lane. Turn R then L at junction,
soon forking R then sharp R at
metal gate, over stile to go L of
paddock. Cross bridge and fork
R to another. Keep forward in
three fields, turning R in
playing field then L at pavilion
to reach road. (Here you
leave poppies).

❺ 6km/3¾ miles
Cross to continue along Mill
Lane. Pass converted mill, L (car
park R), over bridge, then L on
fenced path across Dedham
Lock. Go R to cross road to L
and join bank of River Stour.
Hug river edge to bridge. Cross
and continue with river L to
reach another bridge.

❻ 8.6km/5¼ miles
Cross to Flatford Mill complex
going R to Willy Lott's House
(scene of 'The Haywain').
Retrace your steps, over bridge
going L past weir on raised
track to sluice. Continue
alongside concrete structures
to gate and go L. After gate
turn R at fingerpost to go L on
track to go under bridge.

❼ 11.1km/7 miles
Turn L to return to the
railway station.

CORNWALL
THE LIZARD

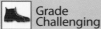

Distance 17.6km/11miles	Time 5½ hours	Grade Challenging

17.6

PLAN YOUR ROUTE

ROUTE
Is it for me? Fields, lanes, coastal footpath
Stiles 11
Suitable for fit walkers

START/PARKING
Car park at Kennack Sands, grid ref SW733165
Nearest town Helston
Refreshments Varied at Cadgwith, Lizard, Ruan Minor
Public toilets Lizard, Cadgwith, Ruan Minor
Public transport None to start

MAPS
Ordnance Survey Explorer 103; Landranger 203 & 204

Looking towards Kennack from the cliffs above the Poltesco Valley.

Photo: Maggie Weston

**Isolated cliffs, a collapsed sea cave, a beautiful valley where serpentine was processed and one of Cornwall's loveliest fishing villages are all to be enjoyed walking to Britain's most southerly point.
By Maggie Weston.**

❶ **Start**
Exit car park, walk back up road, join coastal footpath near top of hill on L. Continue to Cadgwith. At road turn L, walk behind beach. When road turns sharp R inland continue ahead uphill on track, follow coastal path signs. At top of hill turn L, pass between houses then turn L signed Iglewidden and Devils Frying Pan. Continue on coastal path to Lizard passing lighthouse.

❷ **8km/5 miles**
At café behind old lifeboat station turn R, firstly up road then along separated path parallel to road. At road turn L then follow road ahead with thatched cottage, Little Trenoweth, L. At village square turn R by shop along Beacon Terrace. Pass school, turn R signed 'Church Cove'. Continue to church on L, turn L. Walk up lane below churchyard wall. At junction turn R. At top of lane negotiate stile. Continue ahead across field. Descend valley, negotiate stones over stream. Continue up track to T-junction, turn L uphill. At top turn R, continue along side of next two fields, hedge, R. Climb stile on R to exit on to lane.

❸ **10.5km/6½ miles**
Turn L up lane, then R in front of Trethvas Farm House. After 20m climb stone steps to footpath raised between fields.

At end of raised path continue straight ahead across field. Exit into lane, continue ahead to minor road, turn L. Just past Anvoaze Barns on L, turn R along track signed 'public footpath'. Pass church, R, continue down side of field, hedge L. At field corner turn R,

continuing along bottom of field. At next corner continue ahead on path between fields. Pass through kissing-gate, continue straight ahead over next field towards houses.

❹ 12.9km/8 miles
Exit on to road, continue ahead

for 30m. Turn L at Prazegooth signed 'Cadgwith'. Walk down lane. At road turn R downhill. Turn L between cottages signed 'car park', continue up valley. At car park walk ahead to stile. Continue ahead through field to gate at L of small building, then ahead to exit on to road. Turn R over bridge, continue for 70m, turn R by postbox. Just before property at top of lane turn R. Continue along path, exit on to road by chapel.

❺ 15.7km/9¾ miles
Turn L, pass shop, turn immediate L on to footpath between houses. Exit at road, continue ahead downhill passing Poltesco Mill. At T-junction turn R, then straight ahead through National Trust car park. Follow sign for 'Carleon Cove'. At coast turn L along coastal path to return to the start.

HERTFORDSHIRE
IVINGHOE

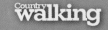

 Distance
16km/10miles

Time
5 hours

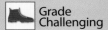 **Grade**
Challenging

SOUTHERN ENGLAND

PLAN YOUR ROUTE

[location map showing Bedfordshire, Buckinghamshire, Hertfordshire and surrounding towns including Newport Pagnell, Biggleswade, Milton Keynes, Brackley, Buckingham, Leighton Buzzard, Letchworth, Hitchin, Stevenage, Dunstable, Luton, UCKINGHAMSHIRE, Aylesbury, Tring, Wendover, Thame, Hemel Hempstead, St Albans, Hatfield, Amersham, Watford, Barnet, High Wycombe, Marlow, Harrow, GREA, Henley, Maidenhead, Uxbridge, Slough, LON, Reading, Windsor, Staines, Richmond, Bracknell, Kingston, Sutton]

ROUTE
Is it for me? Woodland and chalk grassland, moderately hilly. Suitable for reasonably fit adults, children and dogs
Stiles None

START/PARKING
Tring Station, grid ref SP951122 (or Ashridge Visitor Centre)
Nearest town Tring
Refreshments Café at visitor centre, two pubs and a shop at Aldbury
Public toilets Ashridge Visitor Centre
Public transport Frequent trains; numerous buses (not all go to the station but all serve other points on or close to the route) from Berkhamsted, Hemel Hempstead Aylesbury, Watford, Wendover, Luton, etc

MAPS
Ordnance Survey Explorer 181

The view west from Aldbury Nowers Nature Reserve.

Photo: Julie Royle

Astonishingly, just over half an hour after boarding a train at Euston Station you could be stepping out on to the Ridgeway and minutes later be exploring beautiful Aldbury Nowers Nature Reserve as you climb towards Ivinghoe Beacon, which marks the end of the Ridgeway's journey from Wiltshire. Not, of course, that you need start your journey at Euston – easy accessibility from much of south and central England is as much a hallmark of the Chilterns as the chalk grasslands and ancient beechwoods which feature in this gorgeous walk. Much of it is within the 5,000 acres of access land encompassed by the National Trust's Ashridge Estate, so do feel free to vary the route and explore further. By Julie Royle.

❶ Start
Turn R from station on to Ridgeway. Follow frequent waymarks, which guide you through Aldbury Nowers and up on to the Pitstone and Ivinghoe Hills. Cross a road and note the cluster of footpath signs here before the final climb to Beacon Hill summit.

❷ 5km/3 miles
Turn R on Ashridge Estate Boundary Trail (AEBT). Go through a gate and along Beacon Hill to intersect a crosspath. Descend R and return to roadside cluster of footpath signs. Turn L on Icknield Way (also still AEBT), walking across grassland and through woodland to a farm.

❸ 8km/5 miles
Enter farmyard, leaving
Icknield Way. Go L, then R, and
follow farm drive to a road and
cross to another path. Follow it
through woodland to a
junction. Turn L, still on AEBT
(now also Ashridge Cycle
Route). Follow this through
woods, ignoring all turnings, to
eventually reach a clearing
around Bridgewater
Monument and Ashridge
Visitor Centre.

❹ 11km/7 miles
Keep straight on across
clearing, still on AEBT. When
path forks, descend R on
Hertfordshire Way. Turn R at a
junction (green and white
signs) and walk to Aldbury.
Turn L, proceed past village
green, along Trooper Road,
past Valiant Trooper and along
a 'no through road' which
becomes a footpath. Keep
straight on after crossing a
bridleway to reach a gate. Go
diagonally to a road and turn R.
Walk to Grand Union Canal,
pass under bridge 136 and
walk to bridge 135, where
a path rises to road near
Tring Station.

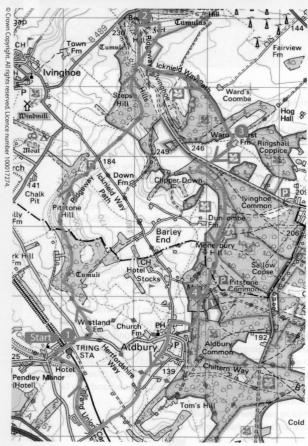

GLOUCESTERSHIRE
NAILSWORTH

Country walking

Distance 14km/8¾miles	**Time** 4½ hours	**Grade** Moderate

PLAN YOUR ROUTE

ROUTE
Is it for me? Pasture, arable and woodland, with some slopes. Suitable for most regular walkers
Stiles 13

START/PARKING
Old Market West, Nailsworth, grid ref ST849996
Nearest town Nailsworth
Refreshments Nailsworth and Weighbridge Inn
Public toilets Bus station, Old Market
Public transport Stagecoach 46 from Cheltenham/Stroud; Stagecoach 93 from Gloucester/Stroud; other local services

MAPS
Ordnance Survey Explorer 168; Landranger 162

The path through Hazel Wood – see Point 2.

Photo: Julie Royle

SOUTHERN ENGLAND

Explore the former mill town of Nailsworth before walking through gorgeous Cotswold woods and pastures, with the opportunity to visit Chavenage House at around the halfway point. By Julie Royle.

❶ Start
Walk along Old Market to Spring Hill, turn R, cross Bridge Street to clock tower and go L on George Street. Cross cattle grid, turn R on Pensile Road, soon with Minchinhampton Common on L. Walk on common if you like but don't lose sight of road. Ignore branching footpaths. Go to R when road forks at Scar Hill. Turn R when footpath crosses road, descend into valley, cross track and proceed through woodland to driveway. Turn L to lane, then turn R.

❷ 1.6km/1 mile
Turn L at Weighbridge Inn, pass Iron Mills then take bridleway on R, climbing through access land to Hazel Wood. Keep straight on at all junctions to top edge of wood. Proceed along green lane, past a field. On returning to woodland, turn L on track. Fork L on bridleway after 500m. Follow bridleway to lane, turn R, soon R again, then L at Woodstock Close, descending to valley bottom. Cross footbridge, turn L through valley then gradually uphill to Avening church.

❸ 5km/3 miles
Go to top R corner of churchyard, through two gates and L past top edge of churchyard. Proceed to lane, turn R, then R on Macmillan Way. After 200m, leave lane on

➤

Horses at West End,
Avening – see Point 3.

L, still on Macmillan Way, which is easily followed across fields to B4014, then across more fields to minor lane. Cross lane then go diagonally across field to hedge/wall corner. Keep to R of hedge/wall, heading towards Chavenage House.

❹ 8km/5 miles
Turn R beside lane, keeping straight on at two junctions. Fork R at Chavenage Green, along north side of green. Turn R at far side, then after 100m fork R on 'restricted byway'. When this bends R, keep straight on into field, descending by L edge at first, then along holloway before swinging L. Go through gate to next field and walk along Ledgemore Bottom, beside wood. At far side of field turn R on concrete track which becomes field edge bridleway. Turn L at junction on hedged track (Longlength Lane).

❺ 12km/7½ miles
Turn L at farm, then R, signed 'public path'. Descend to lane and turn R on to footpath. Pass stables, walk across grassy bank and descend to lane. Turn R, then take first footpath on L. Walk along field edge then straight on along a green lane to meet Tetbury Lane. Descend to A46, cross road and follow Butcher Hills Lane to the Old Market.

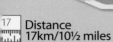

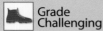

17 Distance
17km/10½ miles

Time
5 hours

Grade
Challenging

PLAN YOUR ROUTE

ROUTE
Is it for me? Farmland and woodland, gently rolling in places but never steep
Stiles 8

START/PARKING
The Square, Stow, grid ref SP192257 (car parks by Fosse Way and Maugersbury Road; bus stop on High Street)
Nearest town Stow
Refreshments Stow, Bleddington, the Oddingtons
Public toilets Stow
Public transport Buses 801 Moreton-Cheltenham to Stow, 855 Moreton-Cirencester-Kemble to Stow; Cotswold Line (Paddington-Great Malvern) trains to Moreton, or to Kingham, just 1km from Bledington

MAPS
Ordnance Survey Explorer OL45; Landranger 163

St Leonard's Church, Bledington – see Point 2.

Photo: Julie Royle

SOUTHERN ENGLAND

Use lovely green lanes and well-maintained field paths to explore the rolling countryside south of Stow, including six delightful villages. By Julie Royle.

❶ **Start**
Walk down Digbeth Street and Park Street then take unsigned footpath to R of Maugersbury Road car park. Descend to a crossroads in Maugersbury and go straight on. Pass Half Moon House then turn R on bridleway. Fork R at Oxleaze Farm and follow bridleway to lane. Turn L, soon L again and then next R into Icomb. Turn L by war memorial, then take a path to R of church. The well-defined path shares a private road at first then runs through fields and young woods, waymarked with blue diamonds of Diamond Way.

Keep straight on at a junction, crossing Oxfordshire Way. After a series of small fields turn R at an unsigned junction to Church Westcote. Turn L through village.

❷ **6km/3¾ miles**
Turn L opposite church, following Diamond Way through fields. Waymarking is patchy here, but if in doubt anywhere just keep straight on. After 1.2km turn L on Seven Shires Way/Diamond Way, following bridleway initially but soon going through gate to take footpath instead. Walk through woodland and scrub, then across fields. Cross Westcote Brook and turn R, joining Oxfordshire Way and continuing across fields to Bledington. Pass church and turn L along a lane. Continue

Blackthorn in bloom near Church Westcote.

across village green and alongside B4450 before taking Oddington bridleway on R. Stay on bridleway at all junctions, ignoring several footpaths and another bridleway which branches R.

❸ 12km/7½ miles
Turn R on meeting a wide track at a major junction, and walk to Lower Oddington. Turn L through both Lower and Upper Oddington. Take a footpath (Macmillan Way) on R after Fox Furlong. Walk along a passageway, diagonally L across a field and through a gate to adjacent field. Walk along R-hand edge to a hedge corner then diagonally to L corner of a reservoir. Proceed along a fenced/hedged path and along edge of playing fields. Leave Macmillan Way when it turns L. Keep straight on instead, then turn L in corner of playing fields and follow waymarked (diverted) path along field edges before cutting across a driveway to road. Turn R, then soon L. Walk to Maugersbury and turn R to Stow.

Distance	Time	Grade
15.2km/9½ miles	5 hours	Moderate

PLAN YOUR ROUTE

Tavy Cleave from Bagga Tor – see Point 4.

Photo: Chris Logan

SOUTHERN ENGLAND

ROUTE

Is it for me? Paths, open moorland and short stretch of country lane. Suitable for all regular walkers. Safety warning: This route enters firing ranges. Check firing times with the national park office (Tel: 01822 890414). Do not touch metal objects. If you see a device, report it to the police
Stiles None

START/PARKING

Lanehead car park, grid ref SX538823
Nearest town Mary Tavy
Refreshments New Inn, Horndon
Public toilets None
Public transport None

MAPS

Ordnance Survey Explorer OL28; Landranger 191

A short stroll beside a leat leads you to the famous Tavy Cleave, a V-shaped gorge aptly known as 'Little Switzerland', where the River Tavy tumbles down rocky falls and chutes for over 3km. Tavy Cleave provides a quick route to Fur Tor, one of the most remote and peaceful high places in England. After taking in the superb panoramic views, follow moorland tracks to join the Lich (or Lych) Way, the eight-mile route used in the 13th-century to carry the dead across the North Moor from Postbridge to Lydford for burial. By Chris Logan.

❶ Start
Turn R beside wall past Nattor Farm and climb to Mine Leat that appears to flow uphill before joining Tavy above a

weir. Follow river to enter deep cleave below Ger Tor but look for a dramatic cascade between boulders into a deep, still pool known as the Devil's Kitchen. Pass below steep edges of Hare Tor before crossing Rattle Brook where river turns R.

❷ 3.2km/2 miles
Climb gently above bracken past range posts and below ruins of Watern Oak Bronze Age village, one of largest ancient settlements on Dartmoor where over 150 people occupied 100 huts and outhouses. Site excavation in 1905 revealed some interesting jewellery amongst a plethora of cooking stones, fragments of pottery and stone arrowheads. Return to riverbank and at Sandy Ford turn L up Amicombe Brook to

cross stream when you reach a long island. Follow next stream to R towards Fur Tor, whose name is derived from Vwr (the great tor) or Feor (the far distant tor). Climb over short grass and between scattered rocks to 572m summit.

❸ 6.4km/4 miles
Enjoy panoramic views before returning towards Sandy Ford down L side of tor on short grass beside clitter. Where ground levels beside stones, angle L and head towards bottom range post other side of Eastern Red Lake, a small stream named after iron-bearing ore that colours its

water. At fifth range post, just before a stream runs down a gully, turn L up grass track parallel to it. Don't miss turning because little more than half-a-kilometre past it lies a perilous area where boundaries of all three firing ranges meet! Circle reeds near top of hill to take track up broad ridge to R.

❹ 12km/7½ miles
Fork R and follow gully through extensive tin and peat workings and past a small cairn below summit of Lynch Tor. Continue parallel to wall before joining Lich Way above Bagga Tor.

❺ 15.2km/9½ miles
Follow track northwards past Brousentor Farm and descend marked path and concrete driveway. Follow footpath to L but keep R on track down to gate on edge of Coffin Wood where corpses carried by packhorse over the wildest and most desolate part of the journey would be placed in coffins. Turn R over wooden bridge beside Cataloo Steps and head towards Higher Willsworthy. Stay alongside river and cross two streams on slatted wooden bridges to climb edge of fields before turning L to cross bridge. Ascend hill and turn R up road to Lanehead.

DEVON
MALMSMEAD

Distance
15km/9¼miles

Time
5 hours

Grade
Moderate

PLAN YOUR ROUTE

ROUTE
Is it for me? One steep ascent and two steep descents. Footpaths, open moorland and quiet lane. Suitable for anyone fit and dogs
Stiles 5

START/PARKING
Lorna Doone Farm, Malmsmead, grid ref SS791478
Nearest town Lynton
Refreshments Pub in Brendon; cafés at start, Cloud Farm, Brendon
Public toilets At start
Public transport None

MAPS
Ordnance Survey Explorer OL9; Landranger 180

A patchwork of green fields on Exmoor.

Photo: Robert Hesketh

SOUTHERN ENGLAND

This classic walk has all the vital Exmoor ingredients: windswept moorland, deep wooded valleys cut by sparkling rivers and a patchwork of green fields with the restless sea beyond. We visit a deserted medieval village, the stronghold of the Doones, that dastardly robber band in R D Blackmore's celebrated 1869 Exmoor novel, 'Lorna Doone'. By Robert Hesketh.

❶ Start
From Lorna Doone Farm take 'Lane Leading to Public Footpath Doone Valley' (or pay 50p and use riverbank path). After 250m, bear L 'Bridleway Doone Valley 2'. At Cloud Farm (teas and lunches) continue ahead 'Bridleway Doone Valley', following the path of the river for 2.5km.

❷ 4km/2½ miles
Just beyond next sign, 'Brendon Common Larkbarrow', path curves R. On L is abandoned medieval village. Its ruins are typical of local longhouses, with one room for farmer's family and one for animals. It has decayed

greatly since 1869 – you need imagination to see the Doones. Return to track, which rises steadily, curving gently away from Hoccombe Combe. When track divides, keep R on better-used fork. Several roughly parallel tracks converge to ford stream at Lankcombe Ford. (At

crossways ahead you may short-cut walk by taking bridleway which cuts north east over Malmsmead Hill, where you turn R and follow Post Lane to start.)

❸ 6.8km/4¼ miles
For full route, continue ahead

'Bridleway Brendon'. Keep ahead 'Bridleway Brendon' at next junction and 'Brendon' when you reach Cross Gate on tarred lane. Descend to village. To visit Stag Hunters Hotel, turn L at Leeford Green, signed 'Simonsbath Barnstaple'. Retrace steps to Leeford Green.

❹ 10.1km/6¼ miles
Turn L 'Lynmouth', cross bridge and turn R, 'Porlock'. Follow lane to stile, 'Footpath County Gate Malmsmead'. Path winds uphill and follows contour over stiles and fields. Cross footbridge and turn L, following curving path uphill. Path divides at top of rise. Keep R on lower path. Go through gate and take lower path R, 'Malmsmead Oare'.

❺ 12.2km/7½ miles
Descend to river. Follow bankside path to second footbridge. Cross and walk up to tarred lane. Turn R and follow lane to start.

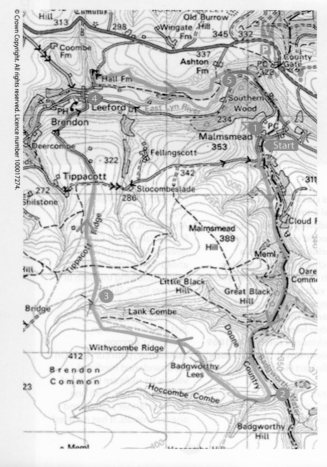

Distance 13.8km/8½ miles	**Time** 4 hours	**Grade** Moderate

PLAN YOUR ROUTE

ROUTE
Is it for me? Good paths, beach; one short, steep climb/scramble
Stiles 9
Suitable for all

START/PARKING
The Rocks Picnic Area, Blackhall Rocks, grid ref NZ471387
Nearest town Peterlee
Refreshments Fish and chip shop/restaurant, café, Blackhall Rocks
Public toilets After caravan site during Point 3
Public transport Bus X35 Hartlepool-Sunderland (connection to Tyneside Metro)

MAPS
Ordnance Survey Explorer 306 & 308; Landranger 88 & 93

Heading along the coastal path at Point 3 of the walk.

Photo: Paul And Christine Monaghan

NORTHERN ENGLAND

The millions of pounds that has gone on reclaiming this area after years of dumping mine waste has proved money well spent. As well as being a fine coastal and beach walk, a number of steep-sided coastal denes are passed. The local soft magnesian limestone erodes easily with the action of water creating the denes, which are home to rare flora and insects. By Paul and Christine Monaghan.

❶ Start
Walk north along road, then take R fork to beach and steps down. Sadly sea erosion has removed sea stacks from this area but a new one is forming at bottom of steps, R. Walk along beach northwards. At end of first stretch, a concrete channel, L, shows site of aerial ropeway featured in film 'Get Carter'. Continue to Castle Eden Dene mouth keeping L of stream.

❷ 2.5km/1½ miles
Near point where outflow stream emerges from dene, ascend steep path up bank side. The surprise view at top is spectacular. Go up steps, L, and return on coastal path which turns R around Blue House Gill. At end of gill, turn L and continue back to start.

❸ 5km/3 miles
Head south on coastal path for 500m. Turn R at stile then L over two stiles and L to steps, R. Descend and ascend steps and turn L around edge of dene. Path swings back to railway arch then returns to cliff edge. Pass caravan site and turn R along road. At main

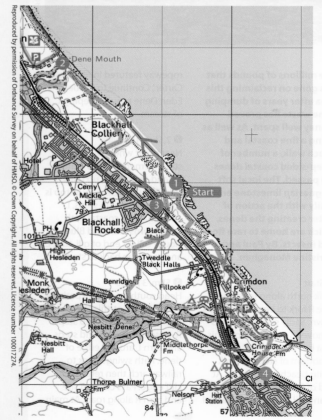

Above, left: A location for the seventies film 'Get Carter' at Point 1.

Above, right: Crimdon Dene viaduct – encountered at Point 3.

road U-turn L into Crimdon Dene. Walk through dene keeping to main path. At wooden bridge at end of dene, deviate L across bridge for 30m for fine view of estuary. Re-cross bridge and go straight on uphill to cycleway and railway bridge. Cross and U-turn R (direction Wingate).

❹ 9.8km/6 miles
Enjoy this path as it crosses dene further on. At a green post, turn R over stile to Blackhall past a pond. Continue past farm to lane. Turn L past Tweddle Children's Animal Farm and R over stile on footpath. Continue along fence, then R over stile towards sea. After next stile, head diagonally L following telegraph poles to stile. Cross road, turn L then R to pass under arch back to start.

13.6
Distance
13.6km/8½ miles

Time
4 hours

Grade
Moderate

PLAN YOUR ROUTE

ROUTE
Is it for me? Terrain Field paths, quiet country lanes, beaches
Stiles 7
Suitable for All

START/PARKING
Car park just above village of Low Newton-by-the-Sea, grid ref NU240248
Nearest town Alnwick
Refreshments Pubs at Low Newton-by-the-Sea, Embleton, Dunstan and Craster; tearooms at Craster
Public toilets Low Newton-by-the-Sea, Embleton and Craster
Public transport Embleton and Craster are served by buses
Accommodation Book a B&B at the 'Book a Bed' section of www.countrywalking.co.uk

MAPS
Ordnance Survey Explorer 332 and 340; Landranger 75

The magnificent sweep of golden sand at Embleton Bay.

Photo: Mark Reid

The magnificent ruins of Dunstanburgh Castle stand silhouetted against the skyline, perhaps the most dramatic castle in Britain. To the north lies Embleton Bay. By Mark Reid.

❶ Start
Walk down towards village. Just before cottages, turn R along lane that runs behind cottages (signpost 'Coast Path'). It turns L to gate leading to track. Follow to Newton Pool Nature Reserve, R. Keep to path alongside hedge and fence of reserve, skirting to R to edge of golf course. Turn R along course boundary on to field. Continue alongside fence then down, fence, L, to wall-stile.

❷ 2km/1¼ miles
Cross wall-stile, then turn L

along field boundary to bridle-gate. Ignore and continue up along fence, L, to top corner of fence. Bear L across field to R-angle corner of field boundary. Head straight across field to wall-stile leading on to road. Turn L into Embleton.

❸ 3.2km/2 miles
Turn L after Dunstanburgh Castle Hotel, then R passing Greys Inn to junction beside Blue Bell Inn. Head towards 'Dunstan, Craster, Howick' then, where cottages end, R, turn L towards 'Dunstan Steads'. Where road bends L take path, R, after Shirewater Low Mill, down over stream, through gate, R, and up to stile in top far field corner. Head straight across field to stile beside gate leading into woods. Follow path to R through woods. Where it

gatehouse. Turn L then R at junction down into Craster.

❺ 7.6km/4¾ miles
Follow road to harbour and turn L along Dunstanburgh Road to bridle-gate at end of road. Follow coastal path straight on for 1.25km to Dunstanburgh Castle. As you approach castle, a path branches off L immediately after gate – follow this across boggy ground beneath rocky outcrops (old moat) then beneath castle ramparts. Path bears R beneath Lilburn Tower to reach coastline again and a gate at Dunstanburgh Castle Golf Course.

❻ 10km/6¼ miles
After gate path divides (beside golf green). Follow path to R, with rocky foreshore, R, passing a pillbox, then continuing over low sand dunes before dropping down to southern end of Embleton Bay. Walk northwards along beach for 750m to Embleton Burn, which cuts through sand dunes. Cross over stream (footbridge slightly upstream), and continue along beach for 1.5km to Low Newton.

divides, head L over footbridge and stile.

❹ 4.4km/2¾ miles
After stile, head R alongside field boundary/hedge, R. Follow path passing plantation on R, just after which, before field boundary bends sharp L, head R over a stile (waymarker)

then bear L and continue straight across fields to gate leading on to lane. Turn L along lane into Dunstan. At road junction, follow road straight on and follow it round to R, then take footpath to L before bus shelter, passing row of houses, R. Follow path across fields to join road near to

LANCASHIRE
WARD'S STONE, BOWLAND

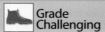

17 Distance
17km/11 miles

Time
5 hours

Grade
Challenging

PLAN YOUR ROUTE

Ambleside •
Coniston •   • Windermere
        Kendal • Sedbergh
⁓m Ulverston   Kirkby Lonsdale
•   • Grange-over-   Ingleton
ness •   Sands   • Carnforth
lney Morecambe •   • Lancaster
sle   Heysham •
                LANCASHIRE
Fleetwood •
      Garstang •
Blackpool •   Clitheroe
    Kirkham •   Burnle⁓
am St Anne's • • Preston   Todr
      Leyland •   Rawtenstall •

ROUTE
Is it for me? Terrain
Gravelled tracks, rough
peaty paths which can
be soggy, tracks, lane
Stiles 1
Suitable for Seasoned
fellwalkers

START/PARKING
Small parking area on
right side of minor road,
east of Stoop's Bridge,
Abbeystead, grid ref
SD563544
Nearest town Lancaster
Refreshments Pubs and
cafés in Lancaster
Public toilets None
Public transport Tel:
Traveline 0870 608 2608
Accommodation
Book a B&B at the
'Book a Bed' section of
www.countrywalking.
co.uk

MAPS
Ordnance Survey
Explorer OL41;
Landranger 102

The view towards Ward's
Stone in the distance

Photo: Jon Sparks / Alamy

NORTHERN ENGLAND

Ward's Stone (561m) is the
highest hill in the Forest of
Bowland and stands
guardian over the city of
Lancaster and Morecambe
Bay. Its broad plateau has
two trig points – one at the
eastern edge where there
are fascinating rock
formations and the other at
the western edge (1m lower)
with even more spectacular
rocks to view.

  Much of the route is not a
right of way but follows
concessionary paths that
cross the grouse moors of
the Duke of Westminster and
these can be closed
occasionally during the
shooting season.
By Mary Welsh.

❶ Start
From parking area, return to
road, turn L, cross bridge and
take waymarked track on R.
Walk ahead and as you near
road at Lower Lee, bear R to
corner, cross footbridge and
then stile. Beyond, turn R to
walk narrow road. Continue to
a junction and take lane
signposted 'Tarnbrook and cul-
de-sac' and walk for 2km to
pass through pretty village
and then go on along
continuing track out on to
low moorland.

❷ 4.5km/2¾ miles
Ignore Wye Way, which turns R,
and keep on, soon to start
your ascent of well-graded
gravelled track as it winds L
and climbs. Carry on along
grassy slopes of Wolfhole Crag
and then teeter along edge of

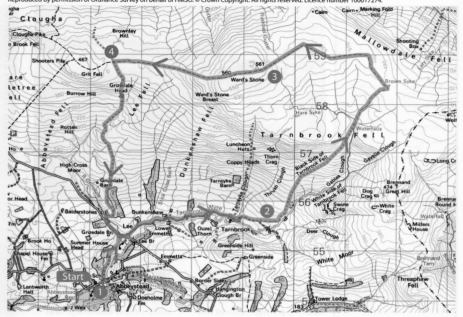

Gables Clough before descending to cross Tarnbrook Wyre on a footbridge. Head on up slope on path and, also where it levels out, to arrive at gateless gap in fence along ridge. Do not pass through but bear L and walk on over large peaty area, keeping boundary always to your R. Follow fence as it climbs fairly steeply and then, when it turns away, follow a narrow path that leads up on to open moorland at eastern edge of hill. Just before commemorative trig point look for Grey Mare with Foal and

the Queen's Chair, fascinating rock structures.

3 11km/6¾ miles
Head on along plateau on dry path to western trig point. Nearby is a huge boulder that gives its name to the fell. Then begin your descent, west, down a narrow peaty path, and then over mirey Cabin Flat, where little path passes through heather. Pick your way carefully and, when at last path disappears, look ahead for two large white notice boards – giving details on the access

strip – and aim for them through the heather.

4 13km/8 miles
Turn L down gravelled track, ignoring any L turns, and after nearly 3.5km, the way passes through pleasing pastures, a great contrast after the wild moorland. Follow waymarks to join narrow lane (taken earlier) where you turn L and descend a hill to take a gate on your R. Walk on ahead to join your outward track and retrace your steps to parking area.

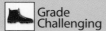
	Distance		Time		Grade
5.7	15.7km/9¾ miles	🕐	5 hours	👢	Challenging

NORTHERN ENGLAND

PLAN YOUR ROUTE

ROUTE

Is it for me? Linear walk on clear paths with some steep sections and stretch of high ridgeline. Navigation can be tricky in bad weather
Stiles 2
Suitable for seasoned walkers

START/PARKING

Broadgate Meadow car park, Grasmere, grid ref NY338077
Nearest town Grasmere
Refreshments Grasmere
Public toilets Grasmere
Public transport Stagecoach 555 from end of walk back to Grasmere. See www.stagecoachbus.com

MAPS

Ordnance Survey Explorer OL5 & OL7; Landranger 90

Walking alongside Grisedale Tarn, Dollywaggon Pike behind.

Photo: Tom Bailey

Take on one of Lakeland's mightiest peaks with this ascent of Helvellyn (950m). Stride up Dollywaggon Pike – its zig-zag path repaired with money raised by CW readers. Then tackle the route back down via Lower Man and Whiteside Bank, watching the brave souls cling to nearby Striding Edge, for views across the whole of Cumbria. Note this is a linear route with a bus trip at the end. By Jenny Walters.

❶ Start
From car park, turn R on B5287, signed 'Windermere/Keswick/A591' and follow to fork in road. Take L to main road, then L again towards Keswick, crossing road and continuing to bus-stop before The Traveller's Rest pub.

❷ 1.1km/¾ mile
Take footpath R up driveway to Winterseeds. Follow path round to L, past buildings and through gate ahead. Swing R across field and through gate, then turn L uphill beside wall and through gate in top L corner. Continue a short distance, then take footpath uphill to R and through kissing-gate in stone wall.

❸ 1.6km/1 mile
Turn L and follow path by wall which starts to bear R, with gill to your L. Go through two gates in quick succession, and follow path round R into valley. Follow clear path along valley, keeping Great Tongue and Tongue Gill on your L, past waterfalls up flagged path through the wall to see Grisedale Tarn.

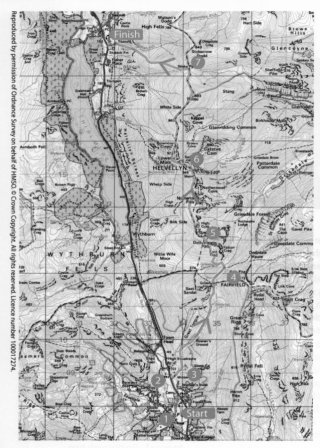

6 9.5km/6 miles
Ignore path to R down Swirral Edge, and continue 450m to Lower Man. Fork R down to pass, then straight on up to top of Whiteside Bank. Fork R again – ignore second fork to R down to Glenridding – and continue on to Raise. Follow path over summit and down to clear path junction at Sticks Pass.

Coming down from Sticks Pass towards the end of your walk.

4 4.8km/3 miles
Take path to R, round tarn, keeping water on your L. Go over stepping stones to base of Dollywaggon Pike. Take path to L and follow zig-zags to summit.

5 7.1km/4½ miles
Follow clear route north (marked with cairns) along ridge, over High Crag and Nethermost Pike to distinctive cross-shaped summit shelter of Helvellyn. Stop for a break, then carry on short distance to the triangulation point.

7 13km/8 miles
Follow path gently downhill, bearing R away from Sticks Gill, then steeply downhill into valley. When you reach a wall, turn R and over footbridge by waterfall, then bear L through gate. Follow path as it bears R and over stile. Turn L downhill and over wall-stile to Tarmac track. Follow to road and turn L to join main road. Turn L on A591 and walk short distance to bus stop.

CUMBRIA
SKIDDAW

Distance
10.9km/6¾ miles

Time
5 hours

Grade
Moderate

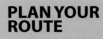

PLAN YOUR ROUTE

ROUTE
Is it for me? Woodland and steep hillsides
Stiles 1
Suitable for fit walkers

START/PARKING
Pay-and-display at Old Sawmill Tearoom, Mirehouse, grid ref NY235281
Nearest town Keswick
Refreshments Old Sawmill Tearoom at start/finish; pubs in Keswick
Public toilets None
Public transport Local bus services 555, X4, 73 and 73A

MAPS
Ordnance Survey Explorer OL4; Landranger 90

Skiddaw Little Man seen from the path across Carl Side.

Photo: Keith Wood

NORTHERN ENGLAND

A fantastic first climb to introduce someone special to the Lakeland heights, but also a sublime way for anyone to explore England's fourth highest mountain. The route rises through the slopes of Dodd Wood to climb Ullock Pike and follow a gentle flank leading on to Skiddaw itself. A steep climb to the summit is rewarded by some of the best views in the Lake District and the gentle descent through the woods is a gem. By Nick Hallissey.

❶ Start
Pass tearoom and enter Dodd Wood, taking path L over bridge, following yellow signs for 'Sandbed Gill Trail'. Visit seasonal osprey viewpoint via detour, R. Continue NW round flank of hill following yellow signs, crossing Sandbed Gill

via bridge. Path joins another then, after 200m, branch R up hill to gate to leave wood and emerge on hillside.

❷ 1.7km/1 mile
Turn R up steep slope and climb to skyline. Main bulk of Skiddaw comes into view ahead. Turn R to join Allerdale Ramble and follow obvious ridge path ('The Edge' on OS map) for steep ascent to summit of Ullock Pike, with occasional zig-zags.

❸ 3.8km/2½ miles
From summit of Ullock, continue over Longside Edge on clear path, crossing Long Side with Skiddaw in fine prospect on L. Path skirts L of Carl Side summit to arrive at Carlside Col, where flank joins Skiddaw. Obvious path runs diagonally up shoulder of

The descent passes heather-clad slopes on the way to Dodd Wood.

Skiddaw, leading directly to middle of summit ridge. On reaching ridge, detour R to south summit for spectacular views over Keswick and Borrowdale, then turn back and head north to main summit. Note – despite path marked on Ordnance Survey Explorer map, there is no safe descent off south summit.

❹ 6.1km/3¾ miles
Retrace steps to cairn marking start of path back down to Carlside Col and turn R to descend. At col, turn L and pass Carlside Tarn. Path descends due south on flank of Carl Side. At 488m, path reaches junction by conspicuous outcrop of white stones (marked on map).

❺ 8.7km/5½ miles
Turn R and take path towards Dodd. Path forks at cairn, turn L and descend to forest road. At road, cross stile and turn R. Follow forest road to fork and keep L, following green marker. Continue downwards, following combination of green and red markers on obvious path towards Bassenthwaite. Path follows course of Skill Beck to return to the tearoom.

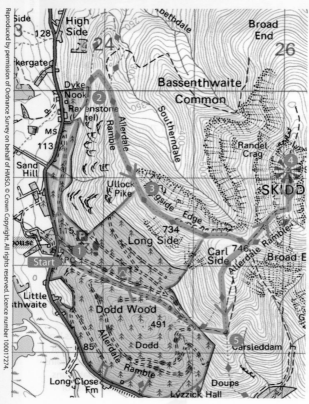

YORKSHIRE
THIXENDALE

Country **walking**

Distance 14km/8¾ miles	**Time** 4 hours	**Grade** Moderate

PLAN YOUR ROUTE

ROUTE
Is it for me? Field paths, bridleways and minor roads; couple of steady climbs plus muddy areas
Stiles 5
Suitable for all

START/PARKING
On roadside near church in Thixendale, grid ref SE843612
Nearest town Malton
Refreshments Village shop and tearoom, Cross Keys, Thixendale; teas at Kirby Underdale post office (seasonal)
Public toilets None
Public transport None

MAPS
Ordnance Survey Explorer 300 & 294; Landranger 106

Heading down into Worm Dale – see Point 5.

Photo: Arnold Underwood

NORTHERN ENGLAND

An ideal walk for the winter months, up over the Wolds into Kirkby Underdale – an unspoilt estate village owned by Lord Halifax of nearby Garrowby Hall. The Norman church is situated in a picturesque setting overlooking Kirby Beck and in early spring the churchyard is a delight firstly with snowdrops, and then daffodils. Thixendale is one of the most charming of the Wolds villages, tucked up in a chalk valley away from the hubbub of the 21st-century. By Arnold Underwood.

❶ Start
Set off due west through village, passing former school/youth hostel now refurbished as village hall. Village shop, on R, has tearoom at rear. Continue along road, passing Manor House. As road swings

R, bear L through gate to follow bridleway into steep-sided dale. Walk up dale for about 1km, then take R fork at gate to climb steadily up to Thixendale Grange. Walk along farm track to road.

❷ 3.2km/2 miles
Turn L along road then look out for signpost indicating path, R, alongside a hedge. Walk down field side. Swing L in next field to keep by hedge and continue more steeply downhill, passing rear of Woodley Farm. At bottom turn L through gate and cross field to join track from farm. Follow track to minor road.

❸ 6km/3¾ miles
Turn L up road for about 100m, and there, cross stile into field on R. Head straight over field, through gate into next and bear R down to footbridge

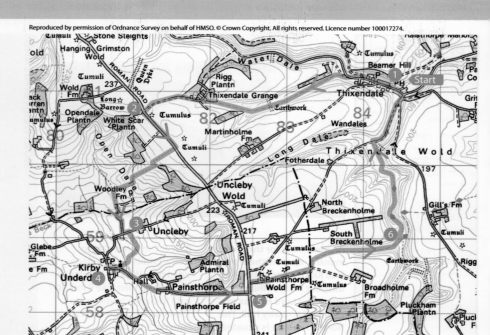

over stream. Continue over next field, heading for Kirby Underdale church and passing an interesting seat carved from a tree-stump. Drop down to stile and footbridge into bottom of churchyard. In spring, banks of stream are brightened by snowdrops, and later, daffodils. To visit village, walk past church entrance up steps on to an enclosed pavement. In village, the little shop/PO may be serving teas and cakes.

❹ 7km/4¼ miles
About turn and walk back down road past church. As road bears L, a footpath crosses a stile, R, and strikes off up hill, passing pond and rear of Painsthorpe Hall. At gate at top another path is met and you continue up past Beech Farm to rejoin Painsthorpe Lane. Plod steadily uphill to a T-junction at top.

❺ 9.5km/6 miles
At road junction, turn L then, in about 200m, R on to a bridleway along farm track. Track heads straight across

Painsthorpe Wold. Leave track where it turns R, and follow bridleway into Worm Dale. Pick your way down to floor of dale and continue to its junction with Thixen Dale. Here several dales and footpaths, including the Wolds Way, converge at a solitary signpost.

❻ 12km/7½ miles
Turn L to follow Wolds Way down dale to road coming down Fotherdale. Go R and walk down road to junction, and there turn L back into Thixendale village.

Distance 11.2km/7 miles	**Time** 3½ hours	**Grade** Moderate

NORTHERN ENGLAND

PLAN YOUR ROUTE

ROUTE
Is it for me? Fields and tracks; one steady climb
Stiles 24
Suitable for all; dogs must be on leads

START/PARKING
Car park by bridge at end of village, grid ref SD911978
Nearest town Reeth
Refreshments Farmers Arms and tearoom, Muker
Public toilets Muker
Public transport Bus 30 from Richmond

MAPS
Ordnance Survey Explorer OL30; Landranger 98 & 91

This walk offers wonderful high and low-level views of Upper Swaledale.

Photo: Andy Latham

Upper Swaledale has its own unique character and is arguably the prettiest of all the Yorkshire dales. The principle attractions in early summer are the glorious wildflower meadows, particularly around the pretty village of Muker. This walk provides a circumnavigation of the impressive hill of Kisdon, offering wonderful high and low-level views of the dale. By Andy Latham.

❶ Start
From car park by bridge, walk along road away from village, then immediately take lane bearing R (Occupation Road). Walk between barns to a T-junction and turn R along ascending track. Climb steadily, enjoying great views of Kisdon, then continue along

a more level section until you cross a small bridge. Turn R to descend a track to a barn then turn L, shortly passing an abandoned farmhouse. Track descends towards some sheep pens but aim to R where a gate gives access to a quaint bridge across a beck. A quick detour through a gate on R gives a good view of a decent waterfall, otherwise continue along track to road. Descend towards Thwaite.

❷ 3.2km/2 miles
Turn R past Kearton Hotel. Head towards an ivy-clad building, pass through stile then through another on L, signed 'Angram'. Skirt barn, through small gate then diagonally across meadow. Pass through damp section alongside stream, gain small ridge by barn. Path continues

▶

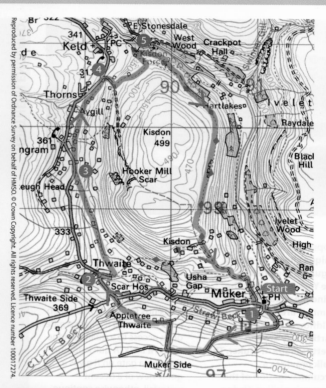

The village of Muker – bathed in glorious evening sunlight.

through succession of stiles, following occasional marker posts, before passing through gate on R to skirt few trees, then climb up slope and aim to R of barn. Continue up to stile giving access to road.

❸ 4.7km/2¾ miles
Go R along road, between two barns, then bear R, through stile, aim for another by barn and signpost for Keld. Pass L of next barn and continue across

pastures through series of stiles and small gates before descending to cross footbridge. Path continues to run parallel to road through many more gated stiles before bearing L to gain access to road. Turn R along road to lane on R, by a barn.

❹ 6km/3½ miles
Descend lane to a ford, then up to junction of tracks by barn. Turn sharp L, pass through couple of gates, and track becomes enclosed to R of barn. After a couple more gates bear L towards sheep pen and follow wall R. At top of steep slope take gate on L, descend field, through stile and then through gate on R to gain good track.

❺ 7.1km/4½ miles
Turn R along track and after short distance a detour can be made on L to descend for view of Kisdon Force. Continuing along track to junction of paths and bear R, following 'Pennine Way' sign. There now follows long traverse of slopes of Kisdon Hill with excellent views down the valley. Go through a couple of squeeze-stiles, and a couple of ladder-stiles, following 'Pennine Way' sign. At second sign, by barn, leave Pennine Way by turning L to descend track. Follow track down to Muker and start of the walk.

0.9 Distance	Time	Grade
10.9km/6¾miles	3½ hours	Moderate

NORTHERN ENGLAND

PLAN YOUR ROUTE

Old Halterburn Head with White Law behind – see Point 3.

Photo: Geoff Holland

ROUTE

Is it for me? Steep ascents and descents; mainly obvious paths and tracks on grassy terrain; one short stretch of Tarmac road
Stiles A number of gates and stiles along the way
Suitable for fit walkers

START/PARKING

Parking on grass alongside Halter Burn, grid ref NT839276
Nearest town Jedburgh
Refreshments Pub in Kirk Yetholm
Public toilets Kirk Yetholm
Public transport None

MAPS

Ordnance Survey Explorer OL16;
Landranger 80

The Cheviot Hills straddle the border between England and Scotland, showing little regard for this arbitrary 'international' boundary. While the majority of the hills lie to the south of the border-hugging Pennine Way, there are a large number of small, green rounded 'Scottish' tops which demand attention. On this walk you'll enjoy a rollercoaster climb over the ridge of Staerough Hill, Sunnyside Hill, Wildgoose Hill and Latchly Hill, before briefly crossing into England. The views throughout are outstanding. By Geoff Holland.

❶ Start
With Halter Burn behind you, cross cattle grid to R and follow road back towards Kirk Yetholm. After 400m, go

through second of two five-bar gates on L and head up hillside towards prominent Staerough Hill. Halfway up join a green track which then diminishes to a path. On flatter ground, go L to triangulation pillar. The view is outstanding. Turn L and, with wall, R, descend to a saddle. Towards end of plantation, where two walls begin to converge, go through gate on L and continue upwards to R. Pass through small gate at junction of two walls and, within 50m, pass through gate, R. Climb diagonally L on a quad track towards wall and fence leading to top of Sunnyside Hill.

❷ 2.8km/1¾ miles
With wall and fence, R, descend to a col, pass through two gates in quick succession and, with wall, R, climb to summit of Wildgoose Hill,

One of the Stob Stones which you will encounter at Point 4.

crowned by Iron Age hillfort. Keeping in same direction, descend to next saddle before climbing steeply to summit of Latchly Hill, highest of four hills making up this high-quality ridge walk.

❸ 4.4km/2¾ miles
Follow dilapidated wall, R, downhill towards Pennine Way alternative route. Just before gate, turn L along clear path to ruins of Old Halterburn Head. Just short of signpost, turn R, cross Halter Burn and head diagonally L uphill on green track to depression between White Law and Steer Rig. Turn L and climb, fence, R, to top of White Law. Fantastic views.

❹ 7.6km/4¾ miles
Turn R through gate in border fence and head downhill to Wideopen Head. At directional fingerpost, turn L through a five-bar gate and continue along track to another gate and a stile. Head straight through and, after 200m, where track begins its downward journey, turn L to reach Stob Stones. Here the gypsy kings and queens were traditionally crowned. Head R to rejoin main track, turning L downhill. This perfect green track is the Pennine Way and eventually leads across the flanks of Green Humbleton to the ford across Halterburn.

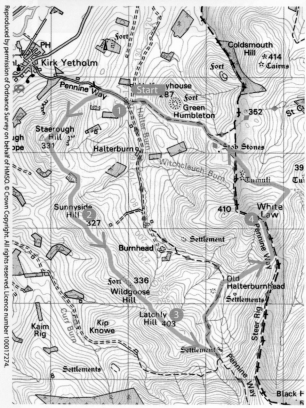

YORKSHIRE
MALHAM COVE

 Distance
10.3km/6½miles

Time
3 hours

Grade
Moderate

PLAN YOUR ROUTE

ROUTE
Is it for me? Clear paths, one steep climb, riverside woodland
Stiles 5
Suitable for all

START/PARKING
Malham Visitor Centre, grid ref SD900627
Nearest town Skipton
Refreshments Pubs and tearooms in Malham
Public toilets Visitor centre car park
Public transport Regular bus links from Skipton and Gargrave

MAPS
Ordnance Survey Explorer OL2; Landranger 98

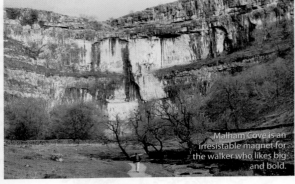

Malham Cove is an irresistible magnet for the walker who likes big and bold.

Photo: Tom Bailey

Deservedly hailed as a 'Wonder of Britain', Malham Cove is an irresistible magnet for the walker who likes their scenery big and bold. From the first view of the vast wall to the climb up on to the limestone pavements above it, the Cove is pure spectacle all the way. Even better, a trip to the Cove also allows scope for a visit to the awesome gorge of Gordale Scar and a visit to the quiet hollows of Janet's Foss. By Nick Hallissey.

❶ Start
From national park car park, join Cove Road heading north through Malham, past Buck Inn. Follow road uphill, past barn. Turn R through kissing-gate signed 'Pennine Way – Malham Cove' and enter Malham Cove Fields. Follow clear path towards Cove, path

soon joining river flowing out from under Cove.

❷ 1.5km/1 mile
As you reach foot of Cove, there are two main options. First is to retrace steps to path, R, leading up western flank of Cove to limestone pavement. Alternatively, cross river and climb slope to east of Cove, then turn L to cross narrow ledge across face of Cove – this rejoins main path up to pavement on western side. Reach limestone pavement and cross, pausing to seek out the edge of Cove and spectacular views.

❸ 2.1km/1¼ miles
Ignore dry valley and cross ladder-stile, following signpost, 'Gordale'. Path diverges, but all routes lead east across flank of Shorkley Hill towards Gordale. Continue

You'll pass this National Trust sign for Janet's Foss at Point 4.

on path for 2km, following signs for Gordale. At road, go through gate and follow road over packhorse bridge to gate, L, and NT sign for Gordale Scar. Continue into Scar.

❹ 4.8km/3 miles
Retrace steps out of Scar and back to road. Turn R, following road round bend, and turn L through gate at NT sign for Janet's Foss (Malham Tarn Estate). Reach waterfall and continue through ravine with river, L. Ravine opens out into meadow, continue on to kissing-gate. Follow past barn and through succession of kissing-gates. At signpost, turn L, signed, 'Pennine Way Hanlith ¾'. Climb hill and pass through kissing-gate. Follow path L of barns, then down steps to join road near Flatts Barn.

❺ 8.5km/5¼ miles
Follow road sharply downhill. Cross river at packhorse bridge then turn R signed for 'Malham'. Follow track to flats. Just before cattle grid, go L through kissing-gate and continue on path past old mill converted into flats and past cattle drinking sump. Cross ladder-stile and follow meadows, crossing brook on footbridge before returning to Malham and start point.

Distance
11.3km/7miles

Time
4 hours

Grade
Moderate

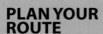

PLAN YOUR ROUTE

ROUTE
Is it for me? Paths, tracks and some trackless ground; lots of rough ground and ups and downs; first part muddy after rain
Stiles 20
Suitable for families with older children (9+); leave the dog at home

START/PARKING
Steel Rigg car park (pay-and-display) at grid ref NY751676 near Twice Brewed
Nearest town Haltwhistle
Refreshments Pub and visitor centre at Twice Brewed
Public toilets None
Public transport None to start

MAPS
Ordnance Survey Explorer OL43; Landranger 86

All ages will find this Hadrian's Wall walk a fascinating journey.

Photo: Steve Goodier

NORTHERN ENGLAND

For kids there's no greater place for stirring the imagination than the border wall that Hadrian draped across the Whin Sill Ridge of Northumberland to mark the northern boundary of the Roman Empire. Our route traverses moorland below the wall to make a rollercoaster return along it past Milecastles and Housesteads Fort. More suited to older children, younger ones with lots of stamina could enjoy it too, and all will find it a fascinating experience. By Steve Goodier.

❶ Start
Exit car park on to road going R downhill to take track R by footpath sign. Cross stile by gate, take track easterly next to wall, L, with crags ahead and Hadrian's Wall above you,

R. Pass plantation, L, and continue past red barn, L, to pass over stile and descend to pass two barns, L. Shortly, leave wall by marker post to cross field and reach stile.

❷ 2km/1¼ miles
Cross stile, go R then L to cross field to stile. Cross, go directly over field to stile. Once over go half-L on cart track, curving R then L to small marker post, R. Leave track, R, heading towards plantation on faint path. Pass L of trees to signpost by old wall and continue ahead along raised ground. Pass lime kiln on R to reach stile. Cross, taking track ahead towards plantation and Bromlee Lough – area very boggy after rain. Pass above lough, reach plantation and pass through via two stiles. Once out, follow path going R when it splits and ascend to gate and stile in Hadrian's Wall.

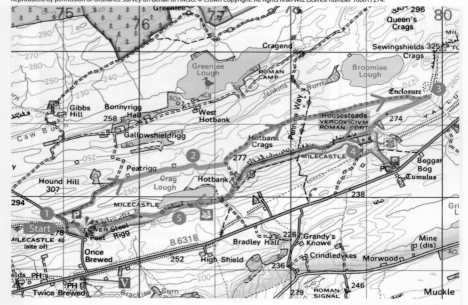

❸ 5.7km/3½ miles
Cross stile going R uphill along Win Sill ridge besides wall. Route-finding is now easy and rollercoaster path follows Hadrian's Wall. Descend finally to trees, cross stile, passing through woods to exit via stone stile, L. Go R descending to Kingsburn Gateway. Go R through kissing-gate then L to ascend steeply to fort at Housesteads, pass on R to reach wooden steps, L.

❹ 6.9km/4¼ miles
Go R taking path through woods below wall, R. Pass through gate to reach open country. Stay by wall as ridge climbs up and down passing a mile castle, R, to finally descend to a deep pass skirting L to avoid crags. Cross stile, heading uphill past Pennine Way stile, R. Continue, eventually descending towards Crag Lough bending L and passing trees, R, to cross two stiles. Bend R by Hotbank Farm to cross stile and farm access road. Cross stile to R going L to cross another stile and climb up through trees steeply, finally exiting at rocky point above lough near Highshield Crags.

❺ 9.5km/6 miles
Pass crags, L, to stile – cross and stay with wall. More ups and downs bring you to Milecastle 39. Continue on ridge to cross stile and carry on, finally curving L to stile, R. Cross, descend very rough steep ground, pass through squeeze-stile and cross boggy level area on slabs. Rise up again leaving path, R, on grassy track just before stile. Ascend by wall, L, going L at wall corner to walk to gate. Pass through, go R to second gate and back to car.

YORKSHIRE
HELMSLEY

Country **walking**

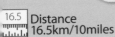

16.5 **Distance**
16.5km/10miles

Time
5 hours

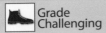

Grade
Challenging

Enjoy the impressive ruins of Rievaulx Abbey at Point 2.

Photo: Arnold Underwood

NORTHERN ENGLAND

PLAN YOUR ROUTE

Peterlee
Hartlepool
Redcar
Middlesbrough Guisborough
gton Stokesley Whitb
Corner
Northallerton
Scalby
Thirsk Pickering
E
Ripon Easingwold Malton

ROUTE
Is it for me? Woodland paths (some indistinct), tracks and country lanes; couple of steep climbs
Stiles 4
Suitable for all – graded 'challenging' due to length of walk.

START/PARKING
Helmsley market square, grid ref SE613838; roadside parking or car park near Helmsley Castle
Nearest town Helmsley
Refreshments Pubs and cafés in Helmsley
Public toilets Helmsley
Public transport Helmsley is served by Scarborough & District 128 from Scarborough (not Sun in winter), Stephenson's 31 from York (not Sun) and Moorsbus from surrounding area

MAPS
Ordnance Survey Explorer OL26; Landranger 100

This is a walk of contrasts – setting off along the well-walked Cleveland Way to the magnificent ruins of Rievaulx Abbey. After this tourist honeypot you will be lucky to meet anyone for the next few miles, as you head off the beaten track through forest down into secluded Beck Dale. Finally, the delightful Ash Dale is followed back down into Helmsley. By Arnold Underwood.

❶ Start
From market square, head north past church, cross B1257 and follow Cleveland Way up lane past main car park, castle ruins, L. Follow Cleveland Way to Rievaulx Bridge. Initially this heads up side of four fields before turning L then R along top edge of woodland. Into woodland, path dips down then up to cross a gully to emerge by a lodge cottage with views down Ryedale. Continue into more woodland, ignoring any other paths and nature trails. Bearing L, descend wooded hillside to minor road, turn L and walk to Rievaulx Bridge.

❷ 4.5km/2¾ miles
Here go R and walk along road to Rievaulx Abbey. With views of impressive ruins, R, continue through village and up hill. Almost opposite church turn L along narrow lane. Do not lose height – keep R at forks in track and woodland gives way to views up Ryedale. At diagonal intersection of tracks, cross straight over to head up and round into open farmland. Track continues alongside a wall to Stokesley road (B1257).

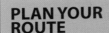

❸ 7.5km/4¾ miles
Cross over, turn L and walk along road for about 800m to gateway to Oscar Park Farm. Turn along farm track to pass through farm. Track swings R to cross dip and up other side. Bear L alongside fence to arrive at gate. Continue along side of next field to another gate leading into extensive forest.

❹ 9.8km/6 miles
Now somewhat off beaten track, footpaths here can be indistinct. Proceed from gate along rutted track. After about 400m track swings L out of dense woodland to meet another track along shallow valley. Turn sharp R here, and, in about 100m look out for waymark on L indicating a

narrow path heading up into trees. This faint path picks its way through trees in easterly direction. Look out for yellow markers pinned to trees. Continue easterly trend, to reach and cross a forest track.

❺ 11.2km/7 miles
Here, land starts to fall away and path descends gradually before bearing L, descent becoming ever steeper. A sharp R continues zig-zag route down into depths of narrow gorge of Beck Dale. Climb to top of eastern side of valley. Now head east away from forest along a field path to minor road. Turn R and then in 200m L to follow a field path into Ash Dale.

❻ 12.8km/8 miles
Walk down dale for about 2km towards Helmsley, keeping to main path, which swings L up to gate. Here you join minor road back into town, turning R at main road to arrive back at market square.

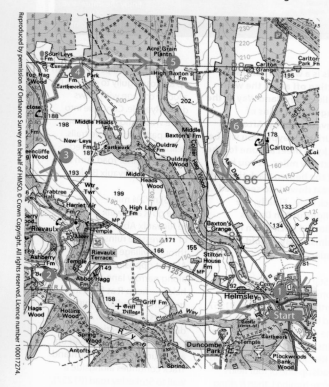

YORKSHIRE
ROSEBERRY TOPPING

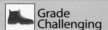

15.5 Distance
15.5km/9¾miles

Time
4½ hours

Grade
Challenging

NORTHERN ENGLAND

PLAN YOUR ROUTE

Redcar
Guisborough
kesley — Whitby
Scalby — Scarborough
Pickering —
Filey
gwold — Malton — Flambon Head
Bridlington
Driffield

ROUTE
Is it for me? Field and moorland paths, tracks and minor roads
Stiles 4
Suitable for Strong walkers – graded 'challenging' due to length of walk.

START/PARKING
Gribdale car park, east of Great Ayton, grid ref NZ592110
Nearest town Stokesley
Refreshments None
Public toilets None
Public transport Arriva NE buses serve Newton-under-Roseberry, from where you can climb Roseberry Topping to join walk at Point 2; Northern Rail Esk Valley trains call at Great Ayton

MAPS
Ordnance Survey Explorer OL26; Landranger 93

A view of Roseberry Topping from Great Ayton Moor.

Photo: Arnold Underwood

A classic walk over undulating heather moorland, taking in the distinctive conical hill of Roseberry Topping, the viewpoint at Highcliffe Nab, and the prominent monument to Captain Cook. By August the moors should be an expanse of purple heather.
By Arnold Underwood.

❶ Start
Head north on Cleveland Way, climbing steeply on to Great Ayton Moor and walk alongside wall. Once past Intake Plantation, Roseberry Topping comes into view, L, over wall. About 2km from start go through gate in wall corner and drop down to Roseberry Common. Continue up the steep steps to the summit (320m).

❷ 2.8km/1¾ miles
Retrace steps down to common where numerous paths radiate through bracken. Take wider path heading diagonally L (north-east). This swings round to enter woodland through which you follow main path for about 1.5km. Path trends gradually down to emerge from trees overlooking parkland. Here cut L, down field to gate and road, opposite entrance to Hutton Hall. Turn R up road towards Hutton village. Large properties border street as far as a gate. Beyond this, a track climbs steadily uphill through the trees.

❸ 6.4km/4 miles
At top keep to main track which doubles back on itself then contours round hillside. A cycle route and the Tees Link path both come this way. Keep

L at a fork (R is to Highcliffe Farm) following main track, which emerges from trees to reveal Highcliff Nab dominating. Go through gate and turn uphill towards crags. When level with crags a path cuts L.

❹ 7.6km/4¾ miles
From crags skirt back round to west. Notice metal signpost, complete with 'rucksack', where Tees Link path leaves Cleveland Way. Head down through trees to gate opening on to a patchwork of fields surrounding Highcliffe Farm.

Follow waymarks through more gates until finally emerging on to moor. Turn R (Cleveland Way) and follow well-trodden path south alongside wall past farm. Continue on main path, which climbs to meet another track on Percy Cross Rigg.

❺ 9.6km/6 miles
Turn L here and follow track along ridge to gate, beyond which commences a Tarmac road. Immediately turn R through another gate and head downhill on track. Capt Cook's monument is now visible in distance above trees on next hill. At bottom, track meets a minor road which you follow straight ahead, up hill and round a bend through trees.

❻ 12.4km/7¾ miles
At top you meet up with Cleveland Way again. Turn R and head due west along wooded fringes of Coate Moor. One final short but sharp climb brings you up on to a plateau upon which sits Captain Cook's monument. From monument head north over Easby Moor and down through woodland to car park in Gribdale.

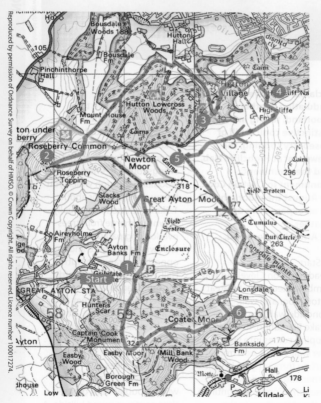

YORKSHIRE
HAWORTH MOOR

Country **walking**

4.5 km	Distance 14.5km/9miles	Time 4½ hours	Grade Moderate

PLAN YOUR ROUTE

ROUTE
Is it for me? Terrain Mostly firm moorland paths; one rougher mile midway round
Stiles 3
Suitable for all

START/PARKING
Church at top of Main Street, Haworth, grid ref SE029371
Nearest town Keighley
Refreshments At start and at Drop Farm, near the end
Public toilets Buses
Public transport Buses from Keighley

MAPS
Ordnance Survey Explorer OL21; Landranger 103 & 104

Looking down over the Worth Valley from Penistone Hill.

Photo: Paul Hannon

As the 19th-century home of the celebrated Bronte sisters, Haworth draws visitors from around the globe. While the majority settle for a potter round the cobbled main street, far better to don your boots and follow Charlotte, Emily and Anne's footsteps out on to the moors. By Paul Hannon.

❶ Start
From front of church, pass round to R to join cobbled road. This runs past Parsonage Museum, and an enclosed path takes over before emerging into fields. Continuing to kissing-gate on to a road on village edge. Go L then bear L up Cemetery Road. This rises on to a corner of Penistone Hill, and it's moorland all the way.

❷ 0.8km/½ mile
At cemetery turn up its near side. Remain on thinner path to top corner, then go R on broader path. Just past far corner is a junction of ways. Go straight on, rising gently L and crossing a plateau to a crossroads with a firm path. Turn R on its level course, ignoring any branches to run on beneath spoilheaps. Before reaching a parking area turn R, a thin path slanting down to cross Moorside Lane to join a rough road at a cattle grid.

❸ 2km/1¼ miles
Turn L along edge of Haworth Moor, the way gradually transforming into a path above valley of South Dean Beck. Path eventually runs down to clapper-style Bronte Bridge. By path immediately before it is the Bronte Chair stone.

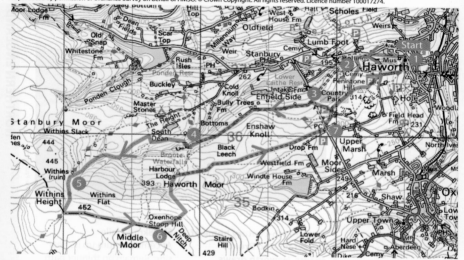

❹ 4.4km/2¾ miles
Cross bridge and ascend bank behind. At kissing-gate path forks: go L, a flagged path slanting up before a long, level section. This passes through one or two pastures before returning to heather moorland. After crossing sidestream it makes a short ascent to junction with Pennine Way. Turn L to Top Withins.

❺ 6.4km/4 miles
Leave on continuing Pennine Way path, which remains stone-flagged as it winds up to watershed. On flat top, moorland skyline of Calderdale appears ahead. Here leave sturdy national trail by a grassy path, L. Within a minute it meets another such way, bear

L along it past a boundary stone. Path now clings to watershed with some inevitably moist moments. Almost at start comes high point of walk, Dick Delf Hill. A gentle dip precedes a slight rise to a boundary stone on Oxenhope Stoop Hill.

❻ 8.8km/5½ miles
Little more than 100m further path reaches a crumbling wall corner. Here leave watershed and follow path L with wall. As you descend look out for a boundary stone at a path junction. Turn L on a thin but clear path traversing moor. The old farm of Harbour Lodge appears below, and path soon slants down towards it. Joining its drive follow it right across

Haworth Moor to ultimately rejoin Moorside Lane, with Drop Farm tearoom, R.

❼ 12.4km/7¾ miles
Turn briefly L, then R on a car park access road. Quickly fork L off this, a short road running to a parking area. Keep straight on firm path ahead, rapidly rejoining outward route. Advance along this and remain on it all the way, ignoring any branches and passing some intriguing 'literary art' before dropping to Dimples Lane. Finally leaving moor, cross straight over and down an access road to Balcony. At bottom keep on down to path junction, where you go L on flagged path to return directly to churchyard.

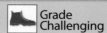

Distance	Time	Grade
14.3km/9miles	7 hours	Challenging

PLAN YOUR ROUTE

ROUTE
Is it for me? Steep mountainsides; paths are clear but very stony; some tricky steps on Corridor Route; one very steep descent at Broad Crag Col
Stiles None
Suitable for fit walkers

START/PARKING
Roadside near Seathwaite farm buildings, grid ref NY235121
Nearest town Keswick
Refreshments Teashop at Seathwaite; pubs in Rosthwaite
Public toilets At start
Public transport Bus service 79 (Borrowdale Rambler) connects Keswick with Seatoller; Seathwaite is 1.7km further down valley

MAPS
Ordnance Survey Explorer OL4 & OL6; Landranger 89

Our 'Peak Fitness' team on the descent from Scafell Pike.

Photo: Matthew Roberts

NORTHERN ENGLAND

The climb to England's highest peak from Seathwaite is one of the finest mountain walks in Britain; the scenery ranges from lush ravines to a serene mountain lake to the rugged shoulders of the high fells. There are spectacular views all around, especially of Great Gable from the Corridor Route. Navigation is straightforward although care must be taken in locating the start of the Corridor Route and the path to Ruddy Gill.
By Nick Hallissey

❶ Start
Head straight on through farm buildings of Seathwaite, passing tearoom, L. Go through gate and follow path heading for far end of valley. Pass through gate and continue to Stockley Bridge which crosses Grains Gill.

❷ 1.4km/¾ mile
Turn R and cross bridge. Pass through gate and take R-hand path at fork, heading uphill. Continue climbing, passing through another gate. Path enters hanging valley above Taylorgill Force and eventually reaches Styhead Gill. Cross stream and continue on bank, stream L, eventually reaching Styhead Tarn. Scafell Pike is now in view directly ahead. Proceed to stretcher box.

❸ 3.9km/2½ miles
At stretcher box, turn sharp L on to cairned path heading towards Great End. Corridor Route now becomes obvious, running along flank of Scafell massif to Lingmell Col, the gap on horizon between Scafell Pike and Lingmell. At large

cairn, turn R and join Corridor Route. Path crosses Skew Gill (a tricky climb out) and later Greta Gill. Path between Greta Gill and Piers Gill includes some rocky outcrops which must be negotiated with care (i.e, possibly on your bottom!). Path climbs to horizon at Lingmell Col, where the view opens out to Wasdale Head and coast.

4 6.6km/4 miles
Turn L at col, making for summit. Path climbs steadily and remains clear all way to summit at 978m (3,210ft), which is marked by an enormous cairn and a trig point. Great views now open out over Scafell, Bowfell and the Langdales.

5 7.5km/4¾ miles
From summit, carefully navigate north-east on to cairned path descending in direction of Broad Crag. Path drops sharply and is badly eroded – care is needed. At Broad Crag Col, path climbs again on to shoulder of Broad Crag, and passes between summits of Broad Crag and Ill Crag. Continue on path, later descending to R of Great End's summit and reaching a prominent cairn at wide, grassy interchange of Esk Hause.

6 9.6km/6 miles
At Esk Hause, turn L on to a clear path snaking back towards Sty Head underneath cliff face of Great End. After 800m, turn R off Sty Head path to cross Ruddy Gill and join path which then follows gill down into Borrowdale. Keep gill L as you descend, until reaching a footbridge where gill and path cross over. Ruddy Gill becomes Grains Gill at this point. Keeping gill R, descend to Stockley Bridge, crossed on ascent. Cross bridge and retrace steps to start.

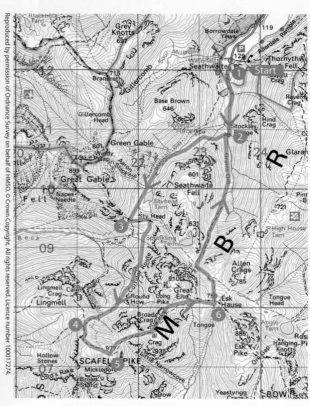

CUMBRIA
LANGDALE PIKES

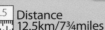 Distance 12.5km/7¾miles	Time 6–7 hours	Grade Challenging

PLAN YOUR ROUTE

ROUTE
Is it for me? Steep paths, exposed fells, some short rocky sections
Stiles 1
Suitable for fit walkers

START/PARKING
Car park near New Dungeon Ghyll Hotel, Great Langdale, grid ref NY295064
Nearest town Ambleside
Refreshments Two pubs, the Old and New Dungeon Ghyll Hotels
Public toilets None
Public transport Bus service 516 connects Ambleside with Great Langdale

MAPS
Ordnance Survey Explorer OL6; Landranger 90

Walk in sheer mountain glory with spectacular views.

Photo: Bob Atkins

Explore five of the most epic and distinctive summits in Lakeland with this magnificent route from Great Langdale. It's sheer mountain glory, taking in the summits of Pavey Ark, Harrison Stickle, Thorn Crag, Loft Crag and Pike o'Stickle, with spectacular views across to Crinkle Crags, Bowfell and Scafell Pike. There are two alternative descents depending on time (and good navigation skills!). By Nick Hallissey.

❶ Start
Walk up access road to New Dungeon Ghyll Hotel. Pass hotel and continue through gate, taking path across meadow and through gap in wall. Follow path across next meadow, passing through gap between two fencelines. Take L-hand path at fork, keeping

wall L. Continue uphill to reach wall running down fellside. Pass through gate and turn sharp R at fork, climbing with wall, R. At next wall, cross stile. Do not cross stream but take R fork, climbing R of crag. Path soon veers L away from wall on to clear path beneath Pike How. Follow path until it levels out just above Pike How. Proceed uphill for 450m then locate grassy traverse branching R across hillside, bringing you to Stickle Tarn.

❷ 1.8km/1 mile
Cross dam and proceed on path, keeping tarn L. Do not follow any path leading directly to cliff face of Pavey Ark. At far end of tarn, follow path heading round eastern side of cliff, crossing two streams and climbing sharply towards north-east side of cliff. Path veers L to North Rake, a

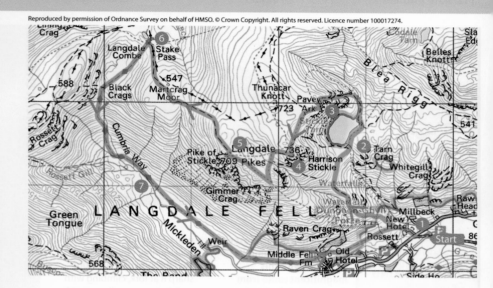

stony channel leading directly upwards. Climb North Rake. At top, turn L at cairn and continue upwards on rough ground to reach summit.

❸ 3.1km/2 miles
Bear south-west from summit to pick up path to Harrison Stickle. Path descends (ignore fork heading L back down to Stickle Tarn) before climbing L of summit crags and reaching summit of Harrison Stickle.

❹ 3.8km/2¼ miles
Head briefly north from summit to locate path descending west into depression between pikes. A path L will take you across Thorn Crag and Loft Crag

summits before reaching Pike o'Stickle, the domed summit at farthest end of depression. Alternatively, you can continue across depression to reach Pike o'Stickle direct (includes stepping stones across bog).

❺ 4.9km/3 miles
Descend from summit and regain path heading north-east. After 1.3km, if a swift descent is desired, branch L at cairn and cross boggy ground to locate top of Troughton Beck. Cross beck and locate steep zig-zag path descending on beck's western side into Mickleden. Path is easy and direct, but is not shown on Ordnance Survey map, so if in doubt, revert to main route. At

valley floor, join Mickleden path and turn L – see Point 7. Path off Pike o'Stickle veers north across Martcrag Moor, eventually reaching a pile of stones at a crossroads of paths. This is the head of Stake Pass.

❻ 6.7km/4¼ miles
Branch sharp L to pick up Cumbria Way, descending on wide, clear path beside Stake Gill, down into Mickleden.

❼ 8.4km/5¼ miles
Follow clear path along bottom of Mickleden, heading south-east and passing Old Dungeon Ghyll Hotel. Continue on path to New Dungeon Ghyll Hotel and retrace steps to start.

6

CUMBRIA
HAYSTACKS

Distance
7.4km/4½miles

Time
3 hours

Grade
Challenging

PLAN YOUR ROUTE

ROUTE
Is it for me? Paths pitched for most of Scarth Gap Pass and partly for ascent of Haystacks
Stiles None
Suitable for seasoned walkers and well-motivated youngsters

START/PARKING
Small pay-and-display car park opposite Gatesgarth Farm at east end of Buttermere, grid ref NY195149
Nearest town Keswick
Refreshments The Fish, the Bridge Hotel and café, Buttermere village
Public toilets Behind The Fish, Buttermere
Public transport Stagecoach Cumberland – Keswick, Buttermere, Whinlatter. Tel: Traveline 0870 608 2608

MAPS
Ordnance Survey Explorer OL4; Landranger 90

The gill down which Black Beck falls to Warnscale Bottom (Point 4).

Photo: Mary Welsh

NORTHERN ENGLAND

This is a 'best day' walk, taking you into the heart of the Lakeland hills. After crossing Warnscale Bottom and ascending the old packhorse route between Buttermere and Wasdale, known as Scarth Gap, a partly pitched path takes you up to the two-cairned, craggy summit of Haystacks. The route continues past two lovely tarns set in a rocky wilderness. The return descent is by a path once used by miners to bring down slate to the valley bottom. By Mary Welsh.

❶ Start
From car park, turn L and, in a few steps, take signposted bridleway on L, just past Gatesgarth Cottages, to walk beside beck. Continue along path, parallel with Buttermere, across valley bottom to cross Peggy's Bridge. Beyond, go through gate and turn R for short way and then turn sharp L to climb well-pitched path up Scarth Gap Pass.

❷ 2.5km/1½ miles
At large cairn on brow of Pass, look for partly pitched path that climbs up, L, towards western face of Haystacks. Near top, scramble up some small crags to two cairns and small nameless tarn.

❸ 3km/1¾ miles
Then go over delightful top, heather-clad and with outcrops, to reach Innominate Tarn, Wainwright's favourite. Another pause here might reveal reflections of Great Gable and Pillar Rock. Go on to pass outflow from Blackbeck Tarn. Follow cairned path as it

Left: The tiny unamed tarn on the summit of Haystacks.

takes you R of Green Crag. Once beyond a path going off R, look for a path descending L.

4 5km/3 miles
Take steepish cairned way. Go past old buildings of disused Green Crag quarry. Here deeply bedded slate was mined; these were known as 'closehead' workings, where slaters worked by candlelight in difficult conditions. Next, look L for a breach in the skyline through which descends Black Beck, crossed earlier. Follow the old quarry path as it descends in a series of zig-zags below the forbidding north face of Haystacks.

5 6km/3¾ miles
Just after a waterfall path takes a sharp turn L and goes down to footbridge over Warnscale Beck. Carry on along an often wet trod to join main track descending, more sedately, from slopes above and bear L along it for 1.4km to return to road and then L to car park.

7

CUMBRIA
NEWLANDS ROUND

Country **walking**

📏 Distance	🕐 Time	🥾 Grade
20km/12miles	6–7 hours	Challenging

PLAN YOUR ROUTE

Cat Bells seen from Maiden Moor with Newlands, left.

Photo: Julie Royle

NORTHERN ENGLAND

ROUTE
Is it for me? Exposed fells, mostly well-defined paths, steep in places
Stiles 2
Suitable for fit adults, keen children and dogs

START/PARKING
Limited parking at Hawes End, at foot of Cat Bells, grid ref NY246211
Nearest town Keswick
Refreshments None
Public toilets None
Public transport Stagecoach 77/77A from Keswick, daily, March–November; also Keswick launch to Hawes End jetty

MAPS
Ordnance Survey Explorer OL4; Landranger 89

You don't have to spend long in Keswick before you hear talk of 'The Newlands Round'. Further investigation reveals that there are nearly as many versions of The Round as there are walkers in Keswick. So this has no pretensions to being The Newlands Round, merely a Newlands Round. But whatever it's called, it's a great walk with stunning views. By Julie Royle.

❶ **Start**
Go through gate above bus stop and cattle grid, walk uphill and cross Grange Road. Turn R to find Cat Bells path, by Skelgill road end. Climb over Skelgill Bank and Cat Bells summit before descending to Hause Gate (a col). Keep straight on, up wide path which soon bears R, rising

easily on to Maiden Moor. Once on top, the path heads south.

❷ **5km/3 miles**
A splendid cairn marks High Spy summit, beyond which path continues south, descending to cross Newlands Beck to Dalehead Tarn, which is followed by steep climb to Dale Head. Another fine cairn marks summit and then path continues along Hindscarth Edge. Hindscarth summit is an obvious detour for peak-baggers, but many walkers will be content to bypass it. Hindscarth Edge soon drops steeply to a col and then rises again as Littledale Edge.

❸ **9.5km/6 miles**
A path veers R, away from adjacent fence, to reach Robinson summit, a rocky

➡

Left: Looking down on Derwent Water from Cat Bells.

outcrop topped by a scrappy cairn. Turn L just after passing summit, on path descending to flat expanse of Buttermere Moss. After prolonged dry weather you can turn R any time after crossing beck at Moss's lowest point. Generally, however, it's wiser to continue on trodden path to High Snockrigg to intercept a path heading towards Newlands Hause. Path is initially faint but then makes a well-defined steep and stony descent well to L of Moss Beck. Cross road at Newlands Hause to a path opposite and climb Knott Rigg.

❹ 13km/8 miles
At top, bear R, crossing series of heathery knolls before descending steeply below Keskadale Farm. Turn L along a lane then take access track to Gill Brow Farm. Approaching farmhouse, turn R down tree-lined track. Cross Keskadale Beck and turn L, then L at next junction. Pass Newlands church and turn R on road. Cross Newlands Beck, pass through Little Town and take a footpath signed to 'Skelgill'. Proceed to Skelgill Farm then turn R to join a track to Hawes End.

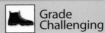
 Distance
14.5km/9miles

 Time
5 hours

Grade
Challenging

PLAN YOUR ROUTE

ROUTE
Is it for me? Exposed fells, mostly good paths, steep in places with loose scree at Windy Gap; you may occasionally need to use your hands for support. Suitable for fit adults, keen children and dogs
Stiles 3

START/PARKING
Honister Hause, grid ref NY225135
Nearest town Keswick
Refreshments Ski Hi Café, Honister Quarry
Public toilets None
Public transport Stagecoach 77/77A from Keswick, daily Mar-early Nov, plus weekend service to nearby Buttermere (via Whinlatter, not Honister) all Nov

MAPS
Ordnance Survey Explorer OL4; Landranger 89

The River Liza with Great Gable in the distance (right).

Photo: Julie Royle

NORTHERN ENGLAND

If you fancy climbing the iconic Great Gable, but dread joining the crowds heading up from Sty Head, this much quieter approach from Honister Hause might be the answer. The views are terrific in all directions, and unusually varied – each valley that you see, and each group of fells, has its own unique character. By Julie Royle.

❶ Start
Take the Grey Knotts path just west of Honister Youth Hostel. Follow signs past quarry and on to open fell. Go steeply uphill, keeping close to a fence. Ignore two stiles but cross a third one. Stay close to fence then turn R in a corner and shortly cross another stile. Bear R over gently undulating ground of Grey Knotts and before long there should be a

fence on your R again. Pass to R of a sizeable pool and ignore a stile. When fence moves to R, keep going straight on to Brandreth summit.

❷ 2km/1¼ miles
From summit cairn, bear very slightly L. Descend to group of pools at Gillercomb Head then

take wide path up Green Gable. Pass two circular stone shelters on top then follow cairns to Windy Gap. Descend steeply on loose scree then tackle steep pull up on to Great Gable. Head north-west across summit to find path descending steeply to Beck Head, where several paths

converge. Turn R on good path and walk to bottom of Windy Gap. Cross a beck then leave main path to follow beck downhill, keeping to R of it. Before long you'll find that the tiny beck has somehow grown into the River Liza.

❸ 7km/4¼ miles
After passing footbridge, climb away from river, passing Black Sail Hut (youth hostel) and proceeding to junction with track through Ennerdale. Fork R uphill to cross Scarth Gap Pass. After crossing summit of Pass, path bears L down Buttermere Fell. Go R when it forks and at bottom go straight ahead on fenced track to Gatesgarth Farm. Pass farm to road and turn R. After a short distance turn R again and take Fleetwith Pike path, beginning with a steep but enjoyable climb up Fleetwith Edge. At top, keep close to edge and you'll eventually meet a bridleway descending to quarry and Honister Hause.

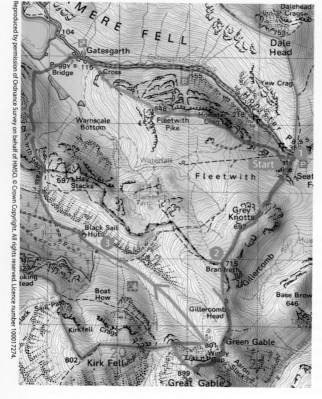

LANCASHIRE
PENDLE HILL

16.2

Distance
16.2km/10miles

Time
5 hours

Grade
Challenging

PLAN YOUR ROUTE

Pendle as seen from above Barley in the evening sun.

Photo: Andy Latham

NORTHERN ENGLAND

ROUTE
Is it for me? Steep ascent, moorland paths, a fine path along the river. Suitable for regular walkers
Stiles 9

START/PARKING
Pendle Inn, Barley, grid ref SD821404
Nearest town Clitheroe
Refreshments Tearooms and pubs in Barley, Chatburn and Clitheroe
Public toilets Barley, Chatburn, Clitheroe
Public transport Pendle Witch Hopper bus P70/71 to Barley from Clitheroe Interchange (Sun only in summer months)

MAPS
Ordnance Survey Explorer OL21; Landranger 103

This connoisseur's route over Pendle starts with the classic ascent from Barley followed by a bracing stroll around the plateau, enjoying outstanding views. The final section along the Ribble to Clitheroe is one of pastoral tranquility. By Andy Latham.

❶ Start
Facing Pendle Inn turn R, pass tearoom and take footpath on L, along stream. Cross bridge and turn L, take L fork then turn R at gate, along cobbled path. Follow stream, coming out by a farm, bear R through kissing-gate then L through another. Cross a dip and climb towards a farmhouse. Proceed behind farm, turn L at wall and after next kissing-gate bear L on a long diagonal uphill. At cairn near top turn R, along edge, to summit trig point.

❷ 3.4km/2 miles
Continue along edge to ladder-stile then take L fork. Cross moor, over ladder-stile and head past large shelter and on to Scout Cairn.

❸ 5.6km/3½ miles
From cairn bear R and begin descending. Cairns mark way down to a rake, bear R for long, slanting descent to wall corner below. Go L at corner, follow wall down then turn R at marker stone. Cross stream and descend alongside next clough to wooden gate by line of trees. Path becomes lane then on to road. Carry straight on along road 'til it bends R and take stile ahead. Cross field, through gate, then another to cross stream. Pass through gate in front of farm and bear L to kissing-gate. Go straight up hill to clear track.

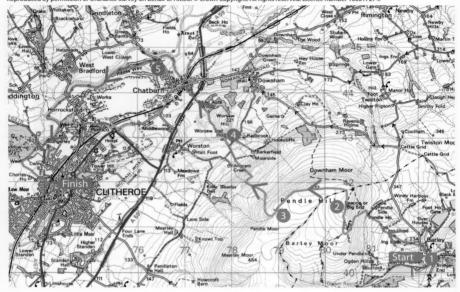

❹ 8km/5 miles
Turn L, skirt base of hill, ascend a rise then descend to wall. Follow this down, cross stile and continue on to A59. Cross and descend through bushes and follow path round garden. Cross another path, follow stream to end, cross bridge and ascend steps. Turn L past church and L over railway down to Chatburn. Turn R along main road then L between school and church. On to a gate in corner of field, on through fields, bearing slightly R and skirting waterworks to reach river. Turn L, follow riverside path which bends back to track and on to the road.

❺ 10.5km/6½ miles
Go L up road then R up steps, through gate and R along Ribble Way. Follow fence and at end of trees descend R to river. Follow river all way to Bradford Bridge. Cross road and continue along riverside path. Pass sign for 'Crosshill Quarry Nature Reserve' and turn R.

Take L fork at compass sculpture and follow main path to eventually meet road. Turn R then L, just before crossing bridge. Continue along river, enter wooded section, climb big steps and at top turn L (second path). On through gate, follow hedge and aim for castle. Take R-hand kissing-gate, bear R to another and gain lane. Turn L, straight on along road, at end turn L, pass station and R through underpass to reach the Clitheroe Interchange.

HIGHLAND
LOCH OSSIAN

Country **walking**

15.3	Distance 15.3km/9½ miles	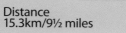 Time 4½ hours	Grade Easy

SCOTLAND

PLAN YOUR ROUTE

ROUTE
Is it for me? Level walking on dry tracks and paths
Stiles None
Suitable for all fit walkers

START/PARKING
Corrour Station, grid ref NN356664
Nearest town Fort William
Refreshments The station restaurant provides excellent meals and also does B&B
Public toilets None
Public transport There are no public roads to Loch Ossian. You will need to reach the start of the walk by taking the West Highland Railway to Corrour Station
Accommodation Book a B&B at the 'Book a Bed' section of www.countrywalking. co.uk

MAPS
Ordnance Survey Explorer 385; Landranger 41 and 42

Loch Ossian is never far away on this walk.

Photo: Stan Pritchard / Alamy

The West Highland Railway Line was opened in 1894 and is one of the most scenic routes in Scotland. Corrour Station, the starting point of this walk, stands on a high, extensive moorland plateau 410m above sea-level, surrounded by dramatic mountains. By Mary Welsh

❶ Start
At Corrour Station, cross railway line and leave station buildings to join estate track, walking east over moorland. Soon lovely Loch Ossian, with its islands and magnificent backdrop of mountains, including Beinn Eibhinn to L and Ben Alder to R, come into view.

❷ 1.5km/1 mile
Pause at T-junction of tracks

and look ahead to see Scottish Youth Hostel tucked snugly under a group of trees. Then turn L to walk on, with a good view down loch. Go through a deer gate beyond which trees have been planted. Follow track as it moves into a plantation of Norway spruce, with faint glimpses of loch through trees. Soon, track comes to edge of water.

❸ 5.8km/3½ miles
Continue close to water. At junction of tracks, turn sharp R to pass a memorial to Sir John Stanley Maxwell (1866-1956) whose research work at Corrour provided the information which led to the afforestation of much of upland Britain. Carry on winding round foot of loch. Pass a boathouse.

HIGHLAND
LOCH OSSIAN

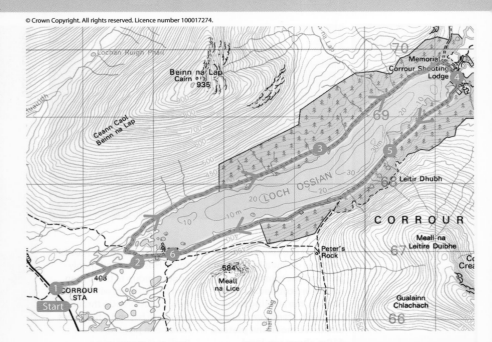

❹ 8.5km/5¼ miles
Cross a substantial burn and where track divides, take R branch. Pass two white cottages and then go on in front of several newly built dwellings. Continue on pleasing track through mixed woodland. Then the delightful, easy-to walk way descends to side of loch and carries on.

❺ 10km/6¼ miles
Go through a gate and stroll on with water lapping beside you.

Deciduous trees clothe steep slopes to your L. Down on shore of loch are little sandy beaches. Carry on to a cross of tracks.

❻ 13.5km/8½ miles
The R one leads to youth hostel, which you might wish to visit. It runs an eco-friendly regime and its site on the edge of the loch is magnificent. The main track carries on to a T-junction of tracks, where you bear L to walk track to station.

The colour purple. Foxgloves flourish by Lake Ossian.

HIGHLAND
KILMARIE

Country **walking**

17
Distance
17km/10½ miles

Time
5–6 hours

Grade
Moderate

PLAN YOUR ROUTE

Loch na Creatheach and the Cuillins from near Point 2.

Photo: Fiona Barltrop

SCOTLAND

ROUTE
Is it for me? Stony moorland track, narrow coast path, quiet roads
Stiles 1
Suitable for most except very young children

START/PARKING
Lay-by on B8083 about 500m past Kilmarie, grid ref NG545173
Nearest town Broadford
Refreshments Shop and café in Elgol
Public toilets None
Public transport Postbus to Elgol. Tel: Traveline 0870 608 2608
Accommodation Book a B&B at the 'Book a Bed' section of www.countrywalking.co.uk

MAPS
Ordnance Survey Explorer 411; Landranger 32

Some of the finest views of the Cuillin Mountains to be found on Skye are those enjoyed from the west coast of the Strathaird Peninsula looking across Loch Scavaig. For even closer views you can take a boat trip from Elgol, and be dropped off at stunning Loch Coruisk to walk back. This circular route uses the coast path along the east side of the peninsula for its return. By Fiona Barltrop.

❶ Start
Getting to the start involves a highly scenic drive from Broadford, passing Beinn na Caillich on your R, then heading round the shores of Loch Slapin in whose waters is reflected the mighty Bla Bheinn. Just beyond Kilmarie there's a parking area on the L. Take the track opposite

(signposted 'Camasunary and Sligachan'). The stony track climbs steadily across open moorland to Am Mam Pass where a dramatic prospect is suddenly revealed: below lies Loch Scavaig and the gentle sandy bay of Camas Fhionnairigh, backed by the savage peaks of the Cuillins, fronted by Sgurr na Stri. To your R is Bla Bheinn's south ridge, while out to sea – beyond small Soay, closest to coast here – the island of Rum dominates the view. Continue on down to Camasunary.

❷ 3.5km/2 miles
From Camasunary follow the coastline (where you'll pick up a path) southwards. Path hugs cliffside and is quite narrow with fairly steep drops on seaward side in one or two places where due care should be taken. The path descends

➡

A view of the Cuillins from near Elgol – see Point 3.

to a stony beach where Glen Scaladal meets the sea. Continue in the same direction, now beneath the crags of Ben Cleat. With every step the scenery becomes ever more spectacular as views of the Cuillins increase. Turn R down road to junction.

❸ 9km/5½ miles
It's worth continuing down road to the jetty, where fishing boats provide an attractive foreground subject, with the distant Cuillins as a backdrop. Return to junction and follow road that runs across moorland to Glasnakille on east side of peninsula. Although it can seem a wrench to leave behind the glorious Cuillins views enjoyed up to now, never fear – there are even more wonderful vistas still to come!

❹ 11km/7 miles
Turn L at junction and follow road, which becomes a track and then a road again. Where road bears L uphill keep ahead on track, turning R on to a path just before a cottage. Continue to meet road that leads you back to Kilmarie and start. There are lovely views along this final section across Loch Slapin and north to Beinn na Caillich.

Distance
18km/11 miles

Time
6 hours

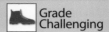
Grade
Challenging

PLAN YOUR ROUTE

SCOTLAND

View across Churchtown Bay, Raasay, towards Ben Tianavaig on Skye.

Photo: Fiona Barltrop

ROUTE
Is it for me? Paths, tracks and quiet roads over moorland and along coast; initially well marked/signposted, Hallaig needs careful navigation
Stiles 3
Suitable for fit adults and older children with stamina

START/PARKING
Sconser ferry terminal on Skye. Walk starts from Raasay pier, grid ref NG554342
Nearest town Portree and Broadford, Skye
Refreshments Isle of Raasay Hotel; Sconser Lodge Hotel, Skye
Public toilets Raasay pier
Public transport Caledonian MacBrayne ferry, Sconser-Raasay, several crossings a day

MAPS
Ordnance Survey Explorer 409; Landranger 24

The lovely island of Raasay is reached by a 15-minute ferry ride from Sconser on Skye: worth every penny for the superb views back to the Skye mountains. If the Cuillins can seem a bit daunting, Raasay's highest point, the flat-topped and comparatively diminutive, if distinctive, Dun Caan, is well within the ability of most walkers. Despite its modest height – 443m – it offers a wonderful panorama. During his Hebridean tour with Samuel Johnson in 1773, Boswell famously danced a reel on the summit! By Fiona Barltrop.

❶ Start
From Raasay pier take path opposite signed for Dun Caan. This follows a dismantled railway incline past ruins of

former iron ore workings, which date back to the First World War. Path enters a forest and crosses a valley; two large piers of railway viaduct still stand. Soon after exiting forest you reach the minor Inverarish-Fearns road.

❷ 2.5km/1½ miles
Opposite is a car park and old mine workings. Follow signs for Burma Road Trail (a reference to its construction by German prisoners of war). About 500m on, Dun Caan is signposted on R. Go up footpath beside Inverarish Burn, which leads over moorland towards Loch na Mna. You can either keep below crags beside loch or go along ridge above. From Loch na Meilich a good path zig-zags up steep grass slopes to craggy summit of Dun Caan.

Left: The evening sky above Glamaig – as seen from the Raasay-Sconser ferry.

❸ 7km/4¼ miles
Simplest and quickest way back is to retrace your steps. For main route, after descending from summit (by the route of ascent) cut L to join path that heads southwards along moorland terrace between Loch na Mna and cliffs on east. When clear of cliffs descend to ruins of Hallaig, a cleared village.

❹ 9km/5½ miles
Path out of Hallaig can be difficult to distinguish. It crosses a burn and goes through woodland, rounding foot of Beinn na Leac. At memorial cairn displaying Sorley MacLean's emotive poem, Hallaig, in both Gaelic and English, the going is much easier.

❺ 10km/6¼ miles
Beyond memorial cairn, path becomes a grassy track that provides a wonderful coast walk (views of Applecross) to the road at North Fearns.

❻ 12.5km/7¾ miles
After first house take a diagonal path downhill to foot of a stream, then follow a path along shoreline to Eyre Point and road back to ferry.

HIGHLAND
ACHNASHELLACH

Country walking

Distance
14km/9 miles

Time
5–6 hours

Grade
Moderate

PLAN YOUR ROUTE

SCOTLAND

A beautiful view over Loch Dughaill, Glen Carron, near the start.

Photo: Fiona Barltrop

ROUTE

Is it for me? Good stalkers' paths; Land Rover and forestry tracks in wild mountain country (take note of signs during deer-stalking season)
Stiles None
Suitable for all with reasonable stamina

START/PARKING

Lay-by on A890 opposite phone box and access road to Achnashellach Station, grid ref NH004484
Nearest town Lochcarron
Refreshments Lochcarron
Public toilets None
Public transport Train or bus (infrequent services) to Achnashellach

MAPS

Ordnance Survey Explorer 429; Landranger 25

Thanks to a number of good stalkers' paths which penetrate the Coulin Forest area that lies between Glen Torridon and Glen Carron in Wester Ross, it's possible to enjoy a taste of some of the Highlands' most impressive mountain landscape without having to be a mountaineering Munro-bagger. Fuar Tholl is a particularly imposing bulk looming above Glen Carron. Also of note are the high ridges of Beinn Liath Mhor and Sgorr Ruadh, which flank the wild valley of Coire Lair into which this walk leads you. Waterfalls and woodland provide a pleasant contrast to the rugged backdrop. The return leg of this route is along a good track over the Coulin Pass, affording fine retrospective views of Beinn Eighe. By Fiona Barltrop.

❶ **Start**
From lay-by go up access road to Achnashellach Station, cross railway and shortly turn L at a forestry track junction. Ahead there is a good view of the prow of Fuar Tholl. Before long take path to L marked with a cairn which leads down to old stalking track by side of River Lair. Walk upstream alongside river, through an attractive area of mixed vegetation: gorse, broom, birch, pines and rhododendrons. You can detour L to view the rocky gorge and waterfalls. As path winds uphill, ground becomes much barer, and the gradient eases as you arrive at wide moorland basin of Coire Lair. Keep R at first path junction to reach a second fork and large cairn 100m further on. Beinn Liath Mhor dominates the view ahead to R.

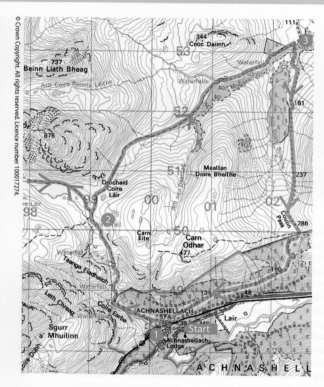

❷ 2.5km/1½ miles

If time and energy permit, it's worthwhile taking L fork here for another 1km towards Loch Coir Lair which lies in an impressive bowl surrounded by Coulin Forest peaks. For main route bear R along path which continues to climb briefly (ignoring another path to L) before descending gently to Easan Dorcha river. Following river down to a small bothy just beyond an impressive waterfall – a lovely spot for a refreshment stop. Continue on down to stone bridge over River Coulin. Look north here for an excellent view of Beinn Eighe.

❸ 7.5km/4¾ miles

Turn R over bridge and follow landrover track which climbs gently south to Coulin Pass. On other side, forestry track leads you back down towards Achnashellach Station and junction near start. Good views of Glen Carron can be had en route. Retrace your initial outward steps.

Left: Easan Dorcha valley and bothy – see Point 2.

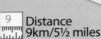

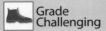

Distance
9km/5½ miles

Time
3 hours

Grade
Challenging

PLAN YOUR ROUTE

Gairloch
Uig · Rona
To·
· Dunvegan
Portree · Raasay · Locha·
Kyle ·
Isle of Skye · Lochal
Kyleaki
Canna · ·Air
Ardvasar· ·

'The Table' – used for hiding cattle and for car advertisements! See Point 2.

Photo: Mary Welsh

ROUTE
Is it for me? Terrain Strenuous walking over rocky and sometimes steep terrain; good boots and waterproof clothing essential
Stiles 1
Suitable for seasoned fellwalkers

START/PARKING
Large parking area (10 cars) on highest point of minor road through pass between Staffin and Uig, grid ref NG444683
Nearest town Portree
Refreshments Nearest at Staffin or Uig
Public toilets Staffin, Uig
Public transport Local bus will drop you off at bottom of pass (Staffin end) and then there is 2.5km climb to start – and also back down!

MAPS
Ordnance Survey Explorer 408; Landranger 23

The Quiraing, the most dramatic part of the Trotternish ridge, lies to the north of the road at the top of the pass between Staffin and Uig. The ridge, huge inland cliffs of volcanic lava, was laid down 60 million years ago. Its eastern slopes are sheer, with landslips and tortured, weathered pinnacles of basalt. The Gaelic name for the Isle of Skye translates as the Isle of Mist, and clouds often envelop the high peaks of the island. This is certainly true of Quiraing where the mists can drift down suddenly. Be prepared to turn back from this challenging, breathtaking walk.
By Mary Welsh.

❶ Start
Cross road, follow good track, north, skirting rocky outcrop.

Carry on with bare hill of Maoladh Mor, L. Continue north-east along inner edge of path to negotiate awkward gully, then go on hugging side of cliff.

❷ 1.5km/1 mile
Path leads to base of sheer face of The Prison, a huge mass of rock. An eroded path leads up, with sheer drop edges – no route for the faint-hearted. Opposite stands The Needle, a huge pillar of basalt, the sides mainly accessible to ravens. Just before pinnacle look for small cairn, L, and follow little path above main path. Ascend steep slope of scree and grass, up through cliffs to reach The Table, a large, oval-shaped bright green table of grass surrounded by towers and pinnacles of rock. This was used for hiding hundreds of cattle from raiders, and in

modern times for a game of shinty and car advertisements! Don't despair if put off by the scree, The Table can be seen from above on this walk but not approached.

Left: 'The Needle' – a huge pillar of basalt to be found at Point 2.

❸ 2.5km/1½ miles
Descend by same route to path. Continue on to ascend short scree slope, then narrow path with steep slopes dropping R. Cross stile over fence and head on, north, along muddy path to high-level small grassy valley, with pretty lochan. Vertical rock faces lie to L and huge heather-clad rocky outcrops to R. Climb path out of glen towards col and cross wall at top. Bear L to cairn.

❹ 4.5km/2¾ miles
Continue bearing L, climbing through gully, then heading southwards towards Meall na Suiramach. Path comes close to cliff edge and you can see dark blue lochans in valley below, also exciting view of The Table, but do not attempt descent.

❺ 5.5km/3½ miles
Walk R on path, uphill, to attain summit cairn of Meall na Suiramach, 543m. Enjoy view then strike south, parallel with cliffs but well inland over moorland. Aim for sheep track through stranded rocks ahead, remaining on the same contour. When clear of cliffs, and you can see parking area far below, descend steep heathery slopes on faint path.

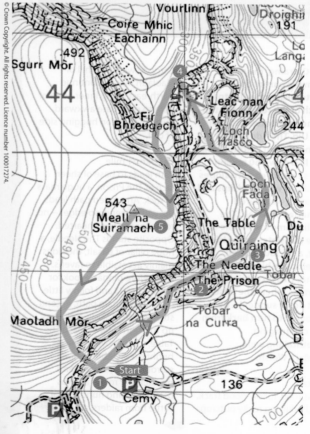

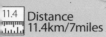
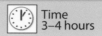

11.4 Distance	Time	Grade
11.4km/7miles	3–4 hours	Moderate

SCOTLAND

PLAN YOUR ROUTE

ROUTE
Is it for me? Old Military Road is a delight in spite of boggy patches; the WHW is wide and reinforced; walking boots essential
Stiles None
Suitable for fit walkers and children with stamina

START/PARKING
Near the access track to Blackrock Cottage, grid ref NN267532 where you immediately join the WHW or White Corries ski centre car park, grid ref NN266526
Nearest town Glencoe
Refreshments Glencoe and Glencoe Visitor Centre
Public toilets Glencoe
Public transport City Link from Fort William or Glasgow stops at the end of the track to either parking area

MAPS
Ordnance Survey Explorer 384; Landranger 41 & 50

Blackrock Cottage is close to the start of your Scottish hike.

Photo: Mary Welsh

Rannoch Moor is a vast expanse of high moorland, interspersed with many boggy patches, pools, lochans, lochs and rivers. Once it was tree-clad and the bleached roots of pines are occasionally seen rising out of the peat. The huge open area has a background of fine mountains. In the depths of winter it is generally too inhospitable to enjoy a walk but on good days, all year round, it can be magical for those who enjoy high-level open spaces. By Mary Welsh.

❶ Start
Join West Highland Way (WHW) and walk due south (R if you have to descend from higher car park and L if you have come by bus)). At Y-junction take R fork, with thistle sign of WHW directing

you along track. Cross a small stone bridge and then leave WHW to walk narrow, sketchy path, R, and go ahead to pick up a better path climbing steadily up moorland. This is the Old Military Road engineered by Major William Caulfield. Work, by 25 officers and nearly 900 men, started on this stretch around 1752. Today it is narrow and occasionally gets lost in bog. Eventually it becomes overlaid by WHW. In high summer path passes through a fine flower garden and your boots crush pungent bog myrtle in wetter areas as it traverses the lower shoulder of Meall a' Bhuiridh – the hill of the bellowing stags! Enjoy magnificent views of Rannoch Moor stretching away in all its grandeur towards mountains. Look for Schiehallion in far distance.

❷ 2km/1¼ miles
At 550m you begin to descend towards distant Wall of Rannoch, a high ridge of mountains, which stands beyond many silvery pools of moor. Way is occasionally lost but continue down until you can join WHW. Turn R and walk

on. Soon after a track leading off L, turn R on another heading R into moorland to now ruinous Ba Cottage, Ba meaning cattle. This must have been a haven when routes over moor were used as drove roads for taking cattle, on the hoof, to markets in south. Return to

WHW and walk on to pass plantation on R and then continue to Ba Bridge over River Ba. This is a delectable spot and one where you will want to linger and enjoy the dramatic gorge where birch and rowan clothe the sides of tempestuous River Ba. The view up-river to the Blackmount hills around the huge corrie is fine.

❸ 6.5km/4 miles
Then begin your return remaining on WHW. Ignore any L or R turns, to arrive at highest point at 443m. Look up L to see a rough unmarked cairn, a memorial to Peter Fleming, author and traveller. Beyond, way continues downhill, is generally easy to walk, and returns you to where you have parked.

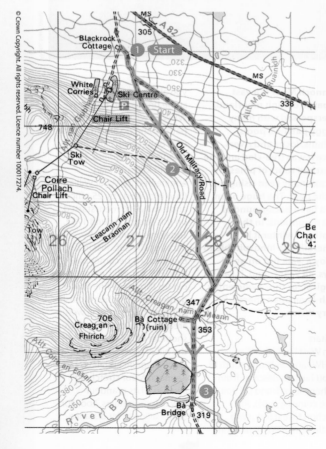

The River Ba from Ba Bridge – you'll arrive here at Point 2.

HIGHLAND
LAIRIG GHRU

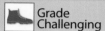

Distance 16.9km/10½miles	**Time** 6 hours	**Grade** Challenging

SCOTLAND

PLAN YOUR ROUTE

ROUTE
Is it for me? Generally good paths and tracks, short section of road walking, some boulder-hopping through the Chalamain Gap
Stiles None
Suitable for fit fellwalkers

START/PARKING
Hay Field car park on road south of Glenmore, grid ref NH980091
Nearest town Aviemore
Refreshments None
Public toilets Nearest at Glenmore
Public transport Highland Country Bus 34 runs from Aviemore to Glenmore

MAPS
Ordnance Survey Explorer 403; Landranger 36

A wild sky to match the wild Scottish countryside.
Photo: Tom Bailey

If wild is what you're after, then it doesn't get much wilder than the Scottish Highlands. Start at Glenmore, clamber over the boulder-strewn Chalamain Gap and down to the Lairig Ghru – a jaw-dropping canyon carved through the eye-widening mountains of the Cairngorms National Park. Ogle the scenery, then meander back through the tamer Glenmore Forest.
By Jenny Walters.

❶ Start
From car park, cross road and walk up L-hand side of road on marked path to Alt Mor car park. At end of car park cross footbridge and take Alt Mor path on R. Follow to road, cross over and take path opposite, keeping road on L and river on R. Continue to footbridge.

❷ 2.3km/1½ miles
Cross footbridge and take path up to R for a short distance, then follow as it turns round hard L. Stick with clear path as it heads south, then bears round to R with river on your L. Keep following – you can see the path snaking into the distance – over a couple of fords and on up to the Chalamain Gap. The going through the gap is very stony so you need to pick your way over the boulders with care.

❸ 5.5km/3½ miles
Continue about 350m beyond the gap, to fork. Take path to L – the route can be boggy and indistinct here. You should be heading diagonally down round hillside to L. Ignore subsequent turn on L heading up to Creag an Leth-choin, and continue downhill until you reach a stream with path beside it.

Left: The path heading from the wilds back towards Glenmore Forest.

❹ 7.2km/4½ miles
You're now gaping into the jaws of the Lairig Ghru! Turn L to explore it further, but you'll have to come out the same way, as the full route through the valley to Braemar is over 20 miles long. So the further you go, the further you'll have to walk back (this mileage isn't included in the route total). To continue, turn R beside stream and follow path round hillside for just over 2km to fork. Take R-hand path, and follow to Rothiemurchus Lodge.

❺ 10.5km/6½ miles
At lodge, turn hard L on forestry track through woodland. Follow as it bears round to R, ignoring any path turnings and sticking with main track until you near the shores of Loch Morlich.

❻ 13.7km/8½ miles
Turn R on track heading SE, then bearing L to stay close to the edge of Loch Morlich – ignore tracks to R taking you south back into the forest. Keep following track, as it heads east away from the loch (ignore footpath turning on L along eastern side of loch) and back to car park.

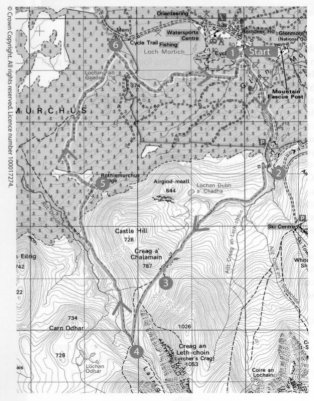

HIGHLAND
BEN NEVIS

4.2
Distance
14.2km/8¾miles

Time
7 hours

Grade
Challenging

PLAN YOUR ROUTE

Shiel Bridge
or
verie   Invergarry•
N
l
Daly
nan•   Spean Bridge•
•Fort William
Oinch•   SCOT
Ballachulish• •Glencoe
e   •Portnacroish
Connel
ane   K

ROUTE
Is it for me? Steep mountainside; paths clear but very stony
Stiles 1
Suitable for fit walkers

START/PARKING
Roadside opposite Glen Nevis Youth Hostel, grid ref NN127717
Nearest town Fort William
Refreshments Pubs and cafés in Fort William
Public toilets None
Public transport Regular bus service (May-Sep) from Fort William bus station to the hostel at Glen Nevis

MAPS
Ordnance Survey Explorer 392; Landranger 41

Get your head in the clouds atop Britain's highest mountain.

Photo: Matthew Roberts

SCOTLAND

Follow in the footsteps of our 'Peak Fitness' team with the classic ascent of Britain's highest mountain. **The Pony Track, or tourist path, is the only safe ascent for a walker, which also makes it the only safe descent. The downsides are that it's very steep, a little monotonous higher up on the 'zig-zag path' and that it's hugely popular at weekends and holidays. You also have to know how to navigate – don't rely on the cairns alone. But you'll be rewarded with stunning views down Glen Nevis and a unique panorama across Scotland from the summit, as well as the triumphant feeling at the top that no-one on British turf is higher than you.** By Nick Hallissey.

❶ Start
Cross River Nevis via footbridge opposite youth hostel. Path turns R; cross stile and follow path across open land to hillside. Path climbs steeply, with some zig-zags, before reaching junction with path ascending from Achintee.

❷ 0.8km/½ mile
Turn R on to this track and proceed up flank of hillside on clear path. Cross two short metal bridges as you climb. Path veers north into ravine separating Meall an t-Suidhe from Ben Nevis. Path zig-zags L then R, entering the corrie containing Lochan Meall an t-Suidhe. Follow path north-east to reach a junction of paths at 600m, just above the lochan.

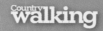

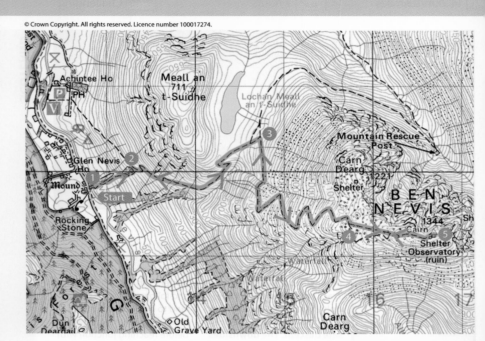

❸ 3km/1¾ miles

Turn R (facing Glen Nevis once more) and head directly for Red Burn, stream dropping sharply from Ben Nevis' summit ridge. Cross burn. This marks start of zig-zags – from here path will carry you clearly up to summit ridge, breaking the gradient with lengthy zig-zags. Several 'short-cuts' have been forged to avoid zig-zags but it's wise to stay on beaten track. At 1,200m, path straightens and makes for summit.

❹ 6.1km/3¾ miles

Path climbs sharply up to summit ridge. Here extreme care must be taken in poor weather, as Ben Nevis' sheer north face drops abruptly away to your L. Path remains clear but can be obscured in snow. Cairns will lead to summit (no other summit path is marked by cairns) but check your course in poor visibility. Summit (1,344m or 4,409ft) includes trig point on high platform and a shelter built into former observatory tower. Well done!

❺ 7.1km/4½ miles

Sadly, only safe descent is via your ascent route. Retrace steps east to find cairned path, again taking great care in poor conditions. Reverse previous instructions to descend to lochan via zig-zags. Turn L above lochan to gain path back into Glen Nevis. About 500m after second metal bridge, watch out for path branching L, leading sharply downhill back to youth hostel.

72

HIGHLAND
TORRIDON

Country **walking**

| 12.8 | Distance 12.8km/8miles | | Time 4 hours | | Grade Challenging |

Walk beneath the western edges of Beinn Eighe at Point 1.

Photo: Ben Winston

SCOTLAND

PLAN YOUR ROUTE

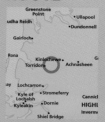

ROUTE
Is it for me? Clear but rough path; wild and exposed mountain moorland; sustained gentle climb
Stiles None
Suitable for fit, suitably equipped walkers (walking boots, waterproofs, map and compass required)

START/PARKING
Car park, grid ref NG958569 Nearest town Kinlochewe
Nearest town Kinlochewe
Refreshments Pubs in Kinlochewe and Torridon; shops in Kinlochewe
Public toilets None
Public transport The Post Bus scheme, tel: 08457 740740 or 01752 387112 for times and fares

MAPS
Ordnance Survey Explorer 433; Landranger 25 & 19

If you ever need an excuse to get out into the wilderness in Scotland without too much effort or bravery, this is it. The walk to Choire Mhic Fhearchair is one of the country's classics, offering wide-open vistas, ancient sandstone mountains, imposing cliffs (you don't go near them!) and an unquantifiable feeling of satisfaction at the end. It's never hard but the terrain can be rough in places, making it ideal for those with sturdy boots and a will to experience how wild this country gets. If you put in the effort with this walk you won't be disappointed. By Ben Winston.

❶ Start
From car park, head down to road and take path L signposted 'Choire Mhic

Nobuil'. After 150m it trends L and begins to climb. It's not steep, but it is sustained. Just over 1km later you begin to enter Coire Dubh Mor and climb relents as you follow path over flatter ground between Liathach and western edges of Beinn Eighe until you reach river.

❷ 2.7km/1½ miles
Cross very carefully on stepping stones (avoid in flood – trekking poles useful) to arrive beneath steep slopes of Coinneach Mhor. Path continues along bottom of coire, rises slightly past a pond, and then climbs gently for 1km until it crosses a stream. In 400m path splits.

❸ 4km/2½ miles
Where path splits, take R fork leading around bottom of Sail Mhor, the enormous

Above: Enjoy a walk in the Scottish wilderness without too much bravery and effort.

mountain, R. Path climbs gently for 700m, then forks again. Take R fork. This now leads north, climbing gently until final climb which brings you rather steeply to Loch Coire Mhic Fhearchair.

4 6.7km/4 miles
If you feel very confident it is possible to circle the loch, but the south side is very rough and pathless and not really recommended. Alternatively, a rough path leads around the north side if you want to get closer to Triple Buttress. Otherwise, turn around and walk back down from the L side of the waterfall and retrace your steps to the car park.

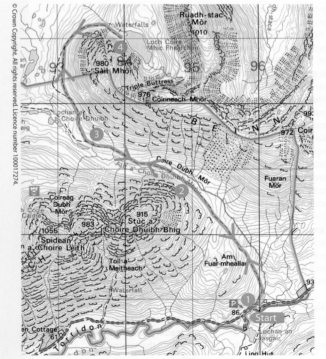

73

HIGHLAND
STAC POLLAIDH

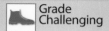

Country **walking**

	Distance 5km/3miles & 2.5km/1½ miles		Time 2 hours & 1½ hours		Grade Challenging

5/2.5

PLAN YOUR ROUTE

uran
Unapool•
Lochinver•
Greenstone Point
•Ullapool
dh
•Dundonnell
che

Stac Pollaidh's two summits are linked by a jagged ridge.

Photo: Mary Welsh

SCOTLAND

ROUTE
Is it for me? Exhilarating climbs on reasonably well-graded routes; walking boots needed; do not attempt in misty weather
Stiles None
Suitable for seasoned walkers

START/PARKING
Car park below Stac Pollaidh, grid ref NC107095; Knockan Cliff, grid ref NC188092
Nearest town Ullapool
Refreshments Ullapool; Achiltibuie
Public toilets Ullapool; Achiltibuie
Public transport For information tel: Ullapool Tourist Information Centre, 01854 612135 or Gairloch Tourist Information Centre, 01445 712130

MAPS
Ordnance Survey Explorer 439; Landranger 15

The distinctive shape of Stac Pollaidh makes it instantly recognisable. Its two craggy summits are linked by a jagged ridge. Because of the excessive erosion caused by the mountain's popularity, together with the fact that it is very steep and composed of sandstone, a reinforced path was put in and this has been re-made and repaired several times. This truly is a magnificent walk and a fabulous viewpoint for the higher peaks of Assynt. By Mary Welsh.

❶ Start
Cross road from car park and follow pitched path through birch to small plateau. Ignore path, L, and continue upwards

from where you can spot the Western Isles. Continue up path, steep but stepped, round east end of hill. Keep to higher path where it divides and climb zig-zags to ridge between two huge rocky outlandish turrets. The view is fantastic. The highest point stands on westernmost end of ridge but requires a difficult scramble and is therefore out of bounds to most walkers.

❷ 2km/1¼ miles
Return almost to top of zig-zags and go on path just below summit to enjoy glorious patchwork of lochs – it's as if you're viewing a relief map.

➡

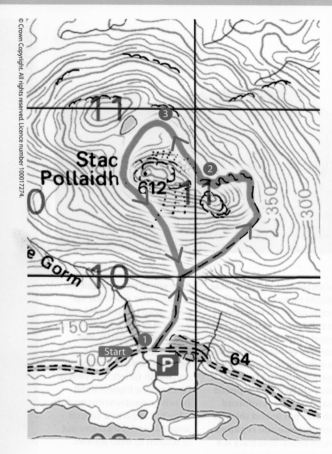

❸ 3km/1¾ miles
At west end of ridge, carry on winding round side of hill as path drops steeply, then traverses south side of hill, soon to descend gently to join main path to car park.

NOTE: To get the full Stac Pollaidh experience, combine your walk with a trip to Knockan Cliff – a wonder and a geological delight. It's seven miles south-east of Stac Pollaidh, on the A835. A walk up to the viewpoint (easily done from the car park) is a must. At one point you can see, through the gap between Cul Mor and Cul Beag, the spectacular shape of Stac Pollaidh.

PERTH & KINROSS
SCHIEHALLION

Country **walking**

SCOTLAND

Distance 10km/6½miles	**Time** 4+ hours	**Grade** Challenging

PLAN YOUR ROUTE

Newtonmore • Kingussie
Laggan • Braema
Dalwhinnie •

OTLAND

PERTH AND KINROSS • Pitlochry
Aberfeldy •
Dunkeld • Bla

Killin •
Lochearnhead
Crieff • Bridge of Earn •
Auchterarder •

ROUTE
Is it for me? Well-made path for first 500m of vertical ascent, then rough boulder-field for remaining climb to summit
Stiles None
Suitable for fit adults, energetic children, dogs on lead

START/PARKING
Large car park at Braes of Foss, just off narrow Schiehallion road running between Loch Kinnardochy and Kinloch Rannoch, grid ref NN753557
Nearest town Kinloch Rannoch
Refreshments Kinloch Rannoch
Public toilets At start
Public transport None

MAPS
Ordnance Survey Explorer 386; Landranger 51 or 42

Schiehallion tops out at a whopping 1,083m (3,553ft).

Photo: Andy Beaven

Schiehallion dominates a huge swathe of Scotland's southern Highlands. Its unmistakeable peak jabs provocatively at the skyline, issuing its challenge to walkers from all points of the compass. It tops out at a whopping 1,083m (3,553ft) and holds a unique place in scientific history. As well as helping 18th-century scientists calculate the mass of the earth, it was also the first mountain ever to be mapped with contours. By Andy Beaven.

❶ Start
From far end of car park, pass through stone gate, past an info board, then on to path. Leaving forestry plantation behind you, L, follow track over heathery slopes on well-made path. Schiehallion rises unmissably on R, although

from here the mountain doesn't resemble the distinctive pyramid you see from the west. Instead you see a long sloping ridge rising to a distant and majestic summit.

❷ 0.5km/¼ mile
After 10 minutes you reach a crossroads where path cuts over a rough vehicle track. On L are solid stone remains of crofters' cottages. From here climb begins in earnest. Conservation charity, The John Muir Trust, bought East Schiehallion in 1999 and began replacing a badly eroded, boggy track with a properly constructed path. Using 3,450 tonnes of aggregate and 400 tonnes of stone (plus £817,000) they built a 3.5km track that zig-zags up the hillside. Purists might argue it detracts from the wilderness experience, but it's definitely a joy to walk on.

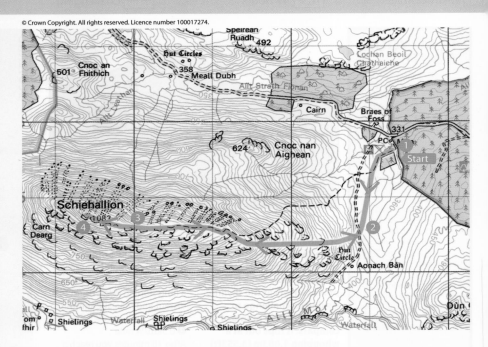

A moderate gradient with sections of rocky steps takes you to a height of around 860m.

❸ 2.5km/1½ miles
All good things must come to an end! The path simply stops where the ground (briefly) flattens out. From here, follow obvious ridge of hill upwards and westwards over the boulder-field. At first, aim for giant cairn jutting into skyline. A faint path picks its way through the rubble, but otherwise it's a case of treading carefully through loose rocks. Beware sprained ankles! Follow

obvious line of broad whaleback ridge as it climbs over a frustrating series of false summits.

❹ 5km/3 miles
Eventually rubble gives way to a series of huge stone blocks and with a quick, easy scramble you're at the top. There's no trig point, but views are magnificent. To the west lies Loch Rannoch, to the east Loch Tummel. To the north are the first giant hills of the Cairngorms; to the south the mighty Glen Lyon Munros. There's no real option for the

return journey but to retrace your steps (taking particular care over the rocks). On the way down, consider this: during a four-month experiment in 1774, scientists dangled weights from strings on either side of Schiehallion and measured how far off vertical they swung. They observed the hill exerted a gravitational pull which they called 'the attraction of mountains'. Luckily, you don't need to be a scientific genius to see the attraction of a hill this good…

75

STIRLING
BEN A'AN

Country **walking**

4.7 **Distance** 4.7km/3miles

Time 2½ hours

Grade Easy

PLAN YOUR ROUTE

ROUTE

Is it for me? Terrain Good path throughout but very rough in places; exposed summit with rocky outcrops – watch kids carefully
Stiles None
Suitable for older children (9+) and leave the dog at home

START/PARKING

Ben A'an car park (free) on south side of A821 near Loch Achray, grid ref NN509070
Nearest town Callander
Refreshments Hotels and café around end of Loch Katrine
Public toilets None
Public transport None, but for Loch Katrine steamers tel: 01877 332000 or Callander Tourist Information, tel: 08707 200628

MAPS

Ordnance Survey Explorer 365; Landranger 57

A view of Ben A'an between Points 2 and 3 of the walk.

Photo: Steve Goodier

SCOTLAND

Don't be fooled by the 'easy' grade and short distance of this up-and-down-the-same-way route. Ben A'an is a Munro in miniature, having all the attributes of a mountain twice the height of its 454m (1,491ft) summit. And don't be worried by returning the same way. This is a route that seems completely different in reverse and besides, there is no other way down, and you can finish off with a steamer ride on wonderful Loch Katrine! As a reward for your efforts you will get a view from the distinct rocky summit that is one of the best in the Highlands. Keep an eye on the kids though – there are crags around the summit. By Steve Goodier.

❶ Start
Leave car park, crossing road carefully by 'Beware Of Traffic' sign and enter 'Queen Elizabeth Forest Park' next to Ben A'an sign. Take good path uphill through trees climbing steeply to reach stone steps. Climb up continuing to more steps and on through trees with burn, R. Go R with path keeping burn R, pass the little waterfalls, R, to climb rougher ground to reach the wooden bridge.

❷ 1km/½ mile
Cross bridge, curve L with path steeply uphill and climb more stone steps. Curve R away from burn continuing ahead and as path levels off, take time to branch L to bench and good rocky viewpoint. Return to main path going L, descend slightly to cross ford continuing uphill on other

Left: Clambering around the summit area of Ben A'an.

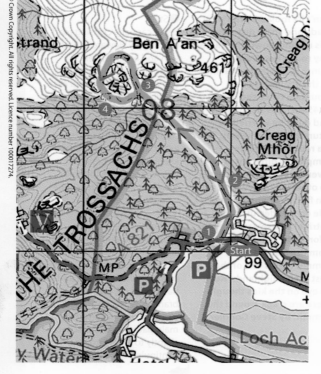

side. Continue through woods crossing muddy area on stepping stones and finally descending through thinning trees towards the distinctive cone of Ben A'an ahead to reach clearing with boulders and viewpoint, L.

❸ 1.9km/1¼ miles
Continue towards rocky steps ascending them steeply to join burn, L, crossing it shortly after to go R next to slabs. Climb rough ground to R of Ben A'an following main path ignoring any L turns. After path levels a little near slabs, L, it climbs again up steps to curve L to back (northern side) of summit. Climb to top staying R when path splits. Take care with kids – summit is rough and rocky.

❹ 2.3km/1½ miles
Return back same way descending roughly to cleared area near boulders (now L). Head into forest following outbound route back down to car park.

76

HIGHLAND
GLEN AFFRIC

Country **walking**

| 17.5 | Distance 17.5km/11miles | Time 4–5 hours | Grade Moderate |

Glen Affric is said to be Scotland's most beautiful glen.

Photo: Andy Beaven

SCOTLAND

PLAN YOUR ROUTE

Kinlochewe • Garve •
Torridon • Achnasheen •

ochcarron •
Kyle of • Stromeferry
ochalsh • Dornie • Cannich •
leakin • HIGHLAND
Shiel Bridge • Invermoristor

• Airor
• Inverie Invergarry •

enfinnan • Spean Bridge •

ROUTE

Is it for me? Easy-to-follow path and track although some sections can be rough or boggy. No steep or sustained ascent or descent. Suitable for fit walkers, older children and dogs on lead
Stiles None

START/PARKING

Large Glen Affric forestry car park at very end of Glen Affric road, grid ref NH284283
Nearest town Kyle of Lochalsh
Refreshments Shop, pubs, hotel in Cannich
Public toilets Glen Affric car park
Public transport None

MAPS

Ordnance Survey Explorer 415; Landranger 25

This walk is a brilliant 'Beginner's Guide to Wild Scotland'. Glen Affric is said to be the most beautiful glen in the country with stunning lochs; unique native Scots woodland of birch, rowan and Caledonian pine; and giant mountains on all sides. It's everything you could want from a Highland wilderness and luckily there's a well-made path that circles the valley bottom making for easy walking amid spectacular scenery. By Andy Beaven.

❶ Start

Even getting to car park is an adventure! A near 13km road winds into Glen Affric from village of Cannich, passing miles of mixed woodland, then glittering waters of Loch Beinn a'Mheadhoin. Eventually road

ends at a forestry car park. Start walking along northernmost track that leaves car park and runs along shore of narrow end of Loch Affric. After 1.5km you reach gates of Affric Lodge. Bear R beside a fence and climb gently away from loch, following path for a further 1km to a kissing-gate in a deer fence.

❷ 2.5km/1½ miles

For next 3km clear but rough path heads west-south-west, climbing gradually from 270m to 330m contour. This stretch is an area of woodland regeneration, fenced off to stop red deer eating young trees. It's part of a bigger project to conserve and extend mixed woodland that once covered huge swathes of Scotland. Among birch and rowan grow magnificent Scots

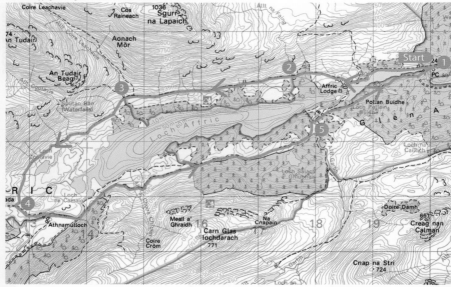

pines with their dark green needles and copper-coloured trunks. Leave this section through another gate. Ignore a turning to R (it's a path up into hills) and continue to a footbridge over tumbling Allt Coire Leachavie burn.

❸ 5.5km/3½ miles
As you follow path south-west, you'll see a waterfall called Sputan Ban cascading off hills to your R. Next you ford the Allt Coulavie, a small river. Normally it only requires a delicate balancing act on stepping stones, but in spate crossing can be tricky. From

here path is less distinct and slightly boggy. Pass small Loch Coulavie, L, and at head of glen path curves south to meet a clearer track at T-junction.

❹ 8.5km/5¼ miles
Turn sharp L and follow track for 500m to bridge over River Affric to Athnamulloch Bothy, a private walkers' hut that was a working croft until as recently as 1950. This is a wonderful place, a flat green meadow surrounded by huge and dramatic mountains. Take track heading east beside river and follow it as it climbs above southern shore of Loch Affric.

Next few kilometres are probably scenic highlight of day with dazzling views north across water into complex ridges and corries of Mam Sodhail (one of the Munros).

❺ 15km/9¼ miles
Cross a bridge over Allt Garbh burn and follow track past a cottage. Soon you see on your L the turreted splendour of Affric Lodge under steep arrowhead of distant Sgurr na Lapaich to north-west. After 2km, turn L at T-junction, then cross a bridge to return to car park. How's that for the full Highland experience?

| 14 | Distance 14km/8¾miles | Time 5 hours | Grade Moderate |

Cape Wrath
Durness
To
Unapool • Altna
Lochinver •

ROUTE
Is it for me? Clear paths, trackless heather, rough path above high cliffs. Full circuit suits only regular walkers with good navigation skills; the out-and-return route to the bay is easier and would suit any fit walker plus dogs on lead
Stiles None, but one fence to be crossed

START/PARKING
Car park Blairmore, grid ref NC195601
Nearest town Kinlochbervie
Refreshments Shop & hotel in Kinlochbervie
Public toilets At start
Public transport None

MAPS
Ordnance Survey Explorer 446; Landranger 9

PLAN YOUR ROUTE

With its beautiful sands and azure sea it could be the Caribbean!

Photo: Len Banister

SCOTLAND

Sandwood Bay is hailed as the most beautiful beach in Scotland. When the sun shines on its white sands, the water shimmers a brilliant azure blue: it's easy to believe you've been whisked from the far north-west of Britain straight to the Caribbean! What makes this place even more special is that you can only reach it by boat… or on foot. An easy path leads 6km from the nearest village and many walkers choose the simple there-and-back option. This route, however, crosses some trackless heather in order to make a circular walk that also includes some invigorating clifftop walking. Of particular interest is The Shepherd (Am Buachaille in Gaelic), a splendid sea-stack that stands guard over the bay. By Andy Beaven.

❶ Start
From small car park in village of Blairmore, walk along to Balchrick then downhill to Sheigra (all 10 houses!). Bear R and climb through village. At last house, road runs out and turns into track. Pass through a gate and carry on across open hillside where Highland cattle graze. Climb steadily then curve L around a small hill called Cnoc Poll a' Mhurain. About 2km from Sheigra, path peters out in shallow valley. From here, bear R (north-east) for 400m over boggy ground and climb on to an unnamed top marked with a cairn.

❷ 3.5km/2¼ miles
From here, eagle-eyed can see a white dot on horizon – Cape

Wrath lighthouse, the most north-westerly point of mainland Britain. Next 1.5km crosses trackless heather: it's slow going, but well worth the effort. Follow a low ridge north for 500m then turn north-north-east across boggy ground. Your target is valley beneath rounded Carn an Righ. Cross stream then fence in bottom of valley, climb steeply for a few metres then turn L on a clear sheep track that heads towards sea. Just before path reaches a rocky bay, turn R and start to climb. Suddenly – wow! You're looking along a wall of 60m-high cliffs. At end stands a lonely sentinel – a sea-stack called The Shepherd (Am Buachaille in Gaelic).

❸ 5km/3 miles
From here, navigation becomes easier as you follow clear path to clifftop. Next 2km offers unrelentingly spectacular walking along cliff edge. Eventually you round a corner for your first view of mile-long Sandwood Bay. At a break in cliffs, path drops down across a grassy slope to beach.

❹ 7.5km/4¾ miles
Return path begins at western end of beach. Go through dunes beneath cliffs of Druim na Buainn. Once on grass, clear path heads south past ruined crofts beside Sandwood Loch. Path is obvious as is climbs away from sea on to moorland past Loch Clais nan Coinneal then Loch Meadhonach to Loch a' Mhuilinn.

❺ 11.5km/7¼ miles
At shore of Loch a' Mhuilinn, path becomes a more substantial track. It climbs southwards for 1km before dropping to shores of Loch na Gainimh. Turn south-west for final 2km back to car park at Blairmore. How's that for a day at the beach?

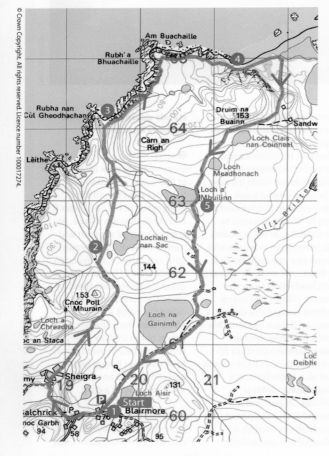

Distance
14.3km/9miles

Time
5 hours

Grade
Challenging

SCOTLAND

PLAN YOUR ROUTE

ROUTE
Is it for me? Long climb up on good paths, though they become indistinct after the Merrick's summit (you can return by the clear outward route if you prefer), with some tricky navigation and tussocky terrain. Suitable for fit hillwalkers
Stiles None

START/PARKING
Car park at end of Loch Trool road, grid ref NX415804
Nearest town Newton Stewart
Refreshments None
Public toilets Nearest at Stroan Bridge, NX371785
Public transport None

MAPS
Ordnance Survey Explorer 318; Landranger 77

On the way up from Loch Trool, not far from the start.

Photo: Tom Bailey

The Merrick is the highest point in the southern uplands of Scotland, a remote top with enormous views over green hills and dales. The path up is clear and easy to follow: you can come down the same way (making a 12.6km or eight-mile hike), or forge your own path over Open Access land on this circular route past lochs, burns and the eerily named Murder Hole.
By Jenny Walters.

❶ Start
From parking area, take path labelled 'Merrick Climb' and follow uphill through kissing-gate and along beside burn. At fork, take path up to L signed 'Please use High Path' and follow to ruined bothy.

❷ 1.8km/1 mile
Continue on path uphill past bothy to junction with forestry track. Turn R, then immediately L, to carry on climbing steeply on path through woods then out on to open hillside. Stick with path through gate in fence and up to wall.

❸ 3.5km/2¼ miles
Turn R uphill beside wall and follow to cairn on Benyellary – and a gorgeous panorama. Continue on path with wall to L, along the Neive of the Spit, keeping straight on when wall curves away to L, over the Broads of the Merrick, and up to the triangulation point on the Merrick summit.

❹ 6.3km/4 miles
Either return the way you came, or if you're feeling adventurous, descend in a

➡

Approaching Loch Valley – see Point 5.

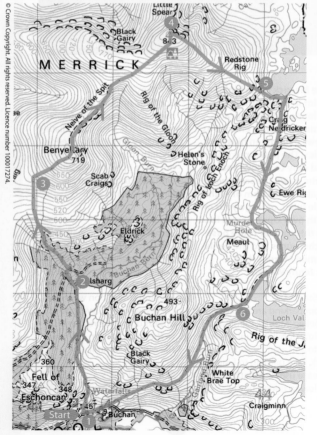

south-easterly direction from summit, down Redstone Rig towards south- west corner of Loch Enoch (grid ref NX440847). There is no clear path, and grassy hillside is bumpy and rough going.

❺ 7.8km/4¾ miles
Head east along southern edge of loch to point where shore swings north, then turn south (away from water) on a vague, and often boggy, path along base of Craig Neldricken. Continue past Loch Arron and lower western slopes of Ewe Rig to west tip of Loch Neldricken (and Murder Hole). Carry on in southerly direction, following path round lochshore – still indistinct and boggy in places – down beside Mid Burn and along western edge of Loch Valley to Gairland Burn.

❻ 11.3km/7 miles
Follow gently downhill beside burn, continuing on path as it bears R away from stream, around hillside, and down through bracken to track. Turn R and follow down to junction with another track, turn R again and follow back to start. (A short detour straight ahead as track bends sharply up to R, will take you to Bruce's Stone and a view down Loch Trool.)

📏 Distance	🕐 Time	👢 Grade
23km/14miles	7 hours	Challenging

PLAN YOUR ROUTE

ROUTE

Is it for me? Clear but rough path most of the way; one section beside Lochan Fada is boggy; final 6km is on easy estate track. This is isolated walking in spectacular mountain scenery far from civilisation! Suitable for fit walkers, dogs on lead
Stiles 2

START/PARKING

Incheril car park 1km east of Kinlochewe, grid ref NH038624
Nearest town Ullapool
Refreshments Village shops, Kinlochewe
Public toilets None
Public transport None

MAPS

Ordnance Survey Explorer 435; Landranger 19

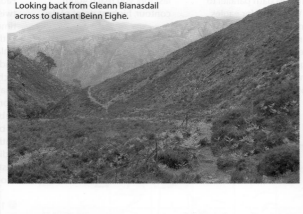

Looking back from Gleann Bianasdail across to distant Beinn Eighe.

Photo: Jennie Webster and Andy Beaven

SCOTLAND

They call it 'The Great Wilderness' – and with good reason. The area to the north of Kinlochewe and Loch Maree is wonderfully rugged and desperately remote. This route allows you to sample this breathtaking back-country while still staying on relatively well-trodden path. It's a long circuit that links picturesque Loch Maree with hidden Lochan Fada. There are mountains everywhere, but this route sticks to the glens. This unrelentingly dramatic landscape is also home to golden eagles.
By Jennie Webster and Andy Beaven.

❶ Start
From Incheril car park 1km east of Kinlochewe, follow path that runs north-west to foot of Slioch. It's easy walking

past fields and woods to shores of Loch Maree, with ever more impressive views of this towering mountain. After around 3km, path splits. Both forks end up in same place but it's easiest to stay by lochside. Where Abhainn an Fhasaigh stream runs down from hills, cross a wooden footbridge, pass through a fence then bear immediately R.

❷ 4.5km/2¾ miles
After 100m a path branches R to a waterfall. Ignore this and keep straight on. After a further 700m path splits beside two cairns. The L fork heads north to climb towards Slioch's summit: a challenge for another day! Instead, head R (north-east) through cliff-walled Gleann Bianasdail. After another 100m, path splits again by a cairn. Keep R on

undulating path parallel to river. Watch out for eagles soaring above Beinn a' Mhuinidh, R. Path becomes rockier and narrower. Midway along glen, cross stream then begin to climb away from river, steeply at first. When 3km from last fork you reach 400m contour, highest point of day.

❸ 9km/5½ miles
View to L is dominated by sharp-pointed summit of Sgurr an Tuill Bhain, Slioch's 934m neighbour. Descend to Lochan

Fada on well-made path that twists and turns, steeply at times. Opposite shore is lined with steep-sided hills – Creag Ghlas Mhor, Meallan a Chruidh and Meallan nan Gobhar. At lochside, cross Abhainn an Fhasaigh stream on stepping stones to reach a beautiful pebbly beach. A cairn at edge of beach marks way ahead. The path becomes boggy and indistinct as it skirts around eastern shore of loch for over a kilometre to a second beach.

❹ 11km/6¾ miles
From here, turn R and follow clear path beneath Sithean Biorach, views R to Loch an Sgeireach and Loch Gleann na Muice. A deer-fence and stile mark edge of Letterewe Estate. After 1.5km into deepening Gleann na Muice, a signpost points L to Dundonnell via either Bealach Gorm or Bealach na Croise. Instead, carry straight on along vehicle track parallel to Abhainn Gleann na Muice stream to a bridge.

❺ 17km/10½ miles
From bridge, it's just over 1km to Heights of Kinlochewe, a tiny settlement. Cross a stile or gate marking end of estate. Ignore track to L, and turn R for final 4km – a pleasant stroll beside Abhainn Bruachaig river through flat-bottomed valley flanked with steep hills and cliffs – back to start.

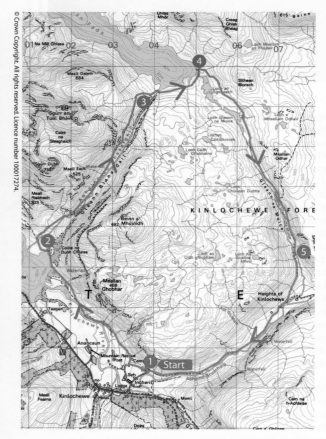

STIRLING
BEN LOMOND

Country **walking**

| Distance 10.5km/6½miles | Time 6 hours | Grade Challenging |

PLAN YOUR ROUTE

ROUTE

Is it for me? Steep, exciting climb, combined with some fine ridge walking. The paths are good

Stiles None

START/PARKING

Large car park at Rowardennan (B837 from Drymen), grid ref NS360987

Nearest town Dumbarton

Refreshments Tarbet, Luss and Rowardennan hotels

Public toilets At start

Public transport No public transport beyond Balmaha. Ferry runs from Apr to Sep from Inverbeg to Rowardennan. For info tel: Traveline 0871 200 2233

MAPS

Ordnance Survey Explorer 364; Landranger 56

Ben Lomond is Scotland's most southerly Munro.

Photo: Mary Welsh

SCOTLAND

Ben Lomond is the most southerly Munro, and stands in an isolated position, dominating the view on the east side of Loch Lomond. It is Glasgow's own mountain and therefore very popular; the tourist route by which this walk descends can be very busy especially at weekends and holidays. The Ptarmigan route is much quieter. By Mary Welsh.

❶ Start
Walk north from car park to sculpture on shore of Loch Lomond. Continue on following West Highland Way (WHW) signs. Take R fork at Y-junction and, beyond gate, go on through deciduous woodland. Ignore track to Ardess. Press on, cross bridge, carry on past NTS Ranger Centre, then white cottage, to cross another burn. Take

narrow path on R, which leaves WHW, and go up through woodland. Beyond gate climb through scattered trees. By old sheepfold go through gate and follow path zig-zagging steeply uphill beside burn. Where path heads away from burn, cross hillside below line of broken crags, then curve up towards ridge. Cross another fence. Carry on up ridge, Tom Fithich, and enjoy views.

❷ 4km/2½ miles
Head on narrowing ridge to subsidiary top, Ptarmigan. Descend to col. Then begin steep, scrambly pull to Ben Lomond's summit.

❸ 5.5km/3½ miles
Leave south-east, on distinct path, along ridge. In 500m veer away from edge of Coire a'Bhathaich and go down steep spur. Continue long,

gradual descent for 2.5km along top of broad spur, Sron Aonaich.

❹ 8km/5 miles
Eventually path curves south-west, comes down through gate and on to edge of forest. Cross Ardess Burn, go through another gate, then follow steep path down forest ride. Finally gradient eases and conifers give way to oak woodland. Continue through trees to car park.

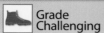
	Distance		Time		Grade
12	12km/7½miles		3–4 hours		Challenging

View from the statue, out over the firth – see Point 2.

Photo: Mary Welsh

SCOTLAND

PLAN YOUR ROUTE

• Drumnadrochit
Grantown-on-Spey
Aviemore •
ewtonmore • • Kingussie
.aggan •
•hinnie •
Braemar •
ΓLAND
• Pitlochry

ROUTE
Is it for me? Mostly good paths through woodland, up heather slopes, over moorland and beside a burn
Stiles None

START/PARKING
Public car park in Fountain Road, Golspie, grid ref NH832000
Nearest town Dornoch
Refreshments Golspie
Public toilets At start
Public transport Golspie reached by National Express and railway. Tel: Traveline 0871 200 2233

MAPS
Ordnance Survey Explorer 441; Landranger 21

Ben Bhraggie is a fine hill and its 30m statue of the 1st Duke of Sutherland stands on the top of a 23m plinth. The statue dominates the skyline, particularly Golspie, the village from where this walk starts, and all his lands around. He was not a good landlord. He drove people off their lands, often burning their houses to make room for a great sheep run. The Big Burn gorge is magnificent. By Mary Welsh.

❶ Start
Walk up Fountain Road. Pass under railway bridge. Go ahead past farm. Wind R, then turn L. Go through deer gate into Ben Bhraggie Wood. Where forest road bends, take signed path, R. Cross forest road and take path ahead. After veering L, close to pylon,

cross two more forest 'roads'. At forest edge, cross another forest road.

❷ 1.5km/1 mile
Ascend narrow path up steep clear-felled slope to reach wooden shelter with splendid view over forest. Take gate beside shelter. Follow steadily rising path through heather, then short steep pull to foot of huge monument on Ben Bhraggie (397m/1,300ft). Beside statue use binoculars to focus on Dunrobin Castle.

❸ 3km/1¾ miles
From back of statue, stride ahead on track through heather moorland, then gently descend round back of hill. At division take lower track descending to deer gate into pine woodland, then beside long boundary wall to R. Just

➡

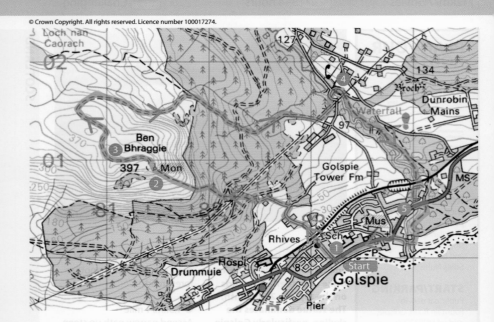

before narrow road, turn L on to winding path through belt of pines. Continue until path drops in large curve to join same road.

❹ 8km/5 miles
Turn L, cross bridge over 'Big Burn'. Bear R, take lower track into woodland, then descend oblique R turn to side of burn. Turn L and walk on. Cross bridge, pausing to look down into huge 'hole' through which

placid burn becomes raging torrent. Continue on path. Before next bridge, bear L through magnificent gorge. Railed paths and railed footbridges lead to platform, projecting into burn below plummeting fall. Return to bridge. Cross. Walk on through gorge, crossing bridges until path climbs steps away from river, on through woodland, to edge of A9.

❺ 10km/6¼ miles
Climb grassy slope, L, over 'Little Bridge' to cross A-road, with care. Go L for three metres, then take narrow path, R, to walk above burn for 500m. At waymark, descend oblique R to stile, then track to road. Bear R to A9, walk L along Golspie main street. Cross at traffic lights, turn L, then R to car park.

16 Distance 16km/10 miles	Time 5 hours	Grade Easy

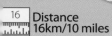

WALES

PLAN YOUR ROUTE

A view across Garreg Ddu reservoir.

Photo: Laurence Main

ROUTE
Is it for me? Cycle track, quiet road, woodland and field paths
Stiles 4
Suitable for all

START/PARKING
Elan Valley Visitor Centre, grid ref SN928646
Nearest town Rhayader
Refreshments Elan Valley Visitor Centre
Public toilets Elan Valley Visitor Centre
Public transport Post bus (Mondays-Fridays) from Llandrindod and Rhayader to Elan Valley Visitor Centre. Buses reach Rhayader from all directions, including bus 63 from Aberystwyth (weekdays only)
Accommodation Book a B&B at the 'Book a Bed' section of www.countrywalking.co.uk

MAPS
Ordnance Survey Explorer 200; Landranger 147

The Elan Valley is the Lake District of Mid-Wales. Its lakes are reservoirs, but they are far too picturesque to be saddled with that label. The visitor centre tells the story of the dams and the railway which enabled their construction around 1900, so that Birmingham could be supplied with water. Follow the line of the old track, then enter woodland to complete a circuit of the lake. The bridge is supported by a submerged dam. Scan the sky for red kites. By Laurence Main.

❶ Start
Walk back along drive from Elan Valley Visitor Centre towards the B4518. When drive narrows, turn sharply L to rise gradually with a grassy path and join a metalled cycle track.

This is the Elan Valley Trail which utilises the course of the dismantled railway and passes the visitor centre, now below you on your L. Walk parallel to a road on your R to reach Caban Coch dam on your L. With the water on your L, continue on edge of Caban Coch reservoir to Carreg Ddu viaduct. This appears to be just a bridge. The submerged dam that supports it ensures that the water level upstream is maintained at a height to allow extraction at Foel Tower, now visible ahead. Cross road to pass this copper-domed tower on your L. The water passes along a 120km aqueduct to Birmingham by gravity. There is a fall of only 52m, making the average gradient 1:2,300. Follow track until it converges with road on your R.

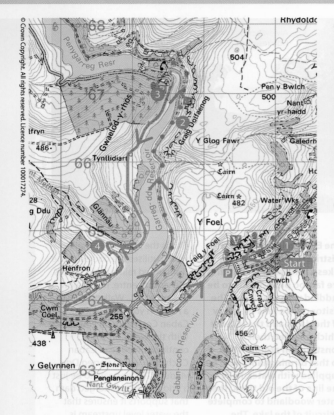

❷ 5.6km/3½ miles
Go ahead, carefully along road. Do not be tempted to climb into the forestry plantation on your R. The top end of this lake is passed on your L, being replaced by the River Elan. Turn L to take bridge across this tumbling river which flows downstream on your L. Continue past car park on your R and come to where road makes a hairpin bend.

❸ 6.8km/4¼ miles
Leaving road to go sharply R, take a gate in the corner ahead and walk along a track below a forestry plantation and above upper reaches of Garreg Ddu reservoir. Come to farm buildings of Tynllidiart and follow waymarked path around back of house and through fields. Continue, as waymarked, through a patch of broadleaved woodland, and descend towards water's edge. Bear R with the path.

❹ 10km/6¼ miles
Follow waymarked path across a stream and through woodland, keeping southern arm of Garreg Ddu reservoir on your L. Approach the viaduct. Turn L across viaduct and admire Garreg Ddu reservoir on your L. On your R is Caban Coch reservoir. Go R to retrace your steps along the Elan Valley Trail to the visitor centre.

POWYS
PONTNEDDFECHAN

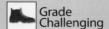

Country **walking**

Distance	**Time**	**Grade**
15km/9¼ miles	5 hours	Challenging

PLAN YOUR ROUTE

WALES

Sgwd Clun-Gwyn waterfall near Point 7.

Photo: Richard Faulks

ROUTE
Is it for me? Forest tracks, some sharp inclines, and very slippery in places
Stiles Several, as well as fallen trees to negotiate
Suitable for: fit, adventurous walkers. Beware slippery rocks when you're near the falls

START/PARKING
In small parking bay, near public toilets, close to Angel pub in Pontneddfechan, grid ref SN901077
Nearest town Neath or Merthyr Tydfil
Refreshments Pubs at Pontneddfechan
Public toilets At start and halfway at Porth Yr Ogof
Public transport Direct bus service from Neath, change buses from Merthyr Tydfil

MAPS
Ordnance Survey Explorer OL12; Landranger 160

Follow this fabulous route for glorious woodland, stunning valleys and awesome waterfalls, with the chance to walk behind the astonishing Sgwd yr Eira. The walk can be slippery and challenging in places, so it's not for the faint-hearted. By Jonathan Manning.

❶ Start
Go through the gate, close to the Angel pub, and follow the clear path up the L side of the river.

❷ 1.75km/1 mile
At junction of rivers, cross first footbridge over the River Nedd Fechan, then follow path on L side of Nedd Fechan, ignoring second footbridge.

❸ 3.7km/2¼ miles
The path passes through a car park and picnic area up to a

road. Turn R on road, then L almost immediately, to continue following river upstream, this time with river on your L.

❹ 5km/3 miles
When you reach a broad track, with metal bridge on L, turn R uphill, signposted to Gwan Bryn-Bwch, leaving river behind you.

❺ 5.5km/3½ miles
At narrow lane, turn R, then in 100m go L at T-junction, still on Tarmac. In 30m, leave road, following path R, signposted Porth Yr Ogof. In 400m look out for blue waymark, and follow waymark L descending sunken lane.

❻ 7km/4½ miles
When path reaches road, turn R towards white visitor centre. If you want to see the

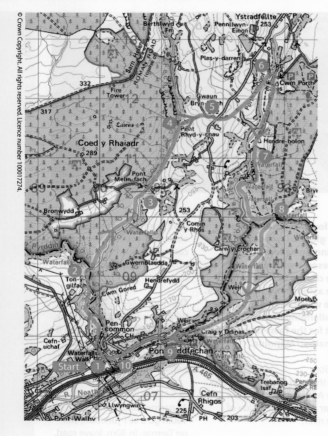

impressive Porth Yr Ogof cave, head into the visitor centre car park and take steps down on L. Otherwise, keep on road, pass visitor centre, L, and take path, R, signed to Sgwd Clun Gwyn.

❼ 8.5km/5¼ miles
At major three-way sign in clearing, go R to Clun Gwyn to see falls, then follow path (clear in parts, indistinct elsewhere) with river, R. The path gradually rises, away from river, eventually joining a broad forest track. Turn R. Follow green waymark diversions to reach waterfalls, then retrace steps to rejoin route.

❽ 10.5km/6½ miles
Look out for fingerpost to Sgwd yr Eira, and follow steps down to river. Turn L to waterfall, and beware slippery path and rocks, especially as you follow path behind the falls. On far side of falls, follow steps to top of the valley.

❾ 10.75km/6¾ miles
At top of valley, follow path R signed to Craig y Dinas. The route skirts, then enters forest. Follow white arrow waymarks ('Advised Route').

❿ 14km/8¾ miles
When you reach Dinas Rock car park, turn R over bridge, and follow quiet residential road back to start point.

PEMBROKESHIRE
NEWGALE–ST DAVIDS

Country **walking**

Distance 15km/9½ miles or 7km/4 miles

🕐 **Time**
5/2 hours

👢 **Grade**
Moderate

PLAN YOUR ROUTE

Strumble Head • C
• Fishguard
Mathry •
St David's • PEMBROKESHIRE
Ramsey Island • Newgale Narberth
Haverfordwest •
Skomer Milford
Island Haven
Skokholm • Neyland
Island Pembroke • • Tenby
St Govan's
Head

ROUTE
Is it for me? Well marked clifftop coast path (national trail), short stretch of Tarmac at end
Stiles 5
Suitable for all except young children

START/PARKING
Newgale, by café, grid ref SM847224 (car parks at Newgale Sands, St David's and Solva)
Nearest town St David's
Refreshments Solva and St David's
Public toilets Newgale Sands, Solva and St David's
Public transport 411 bus every hour from St David's to Newgale via Solva
Accommodation Fishguard Bay Caravan & Camping Park, tel: 01348 811415, www.fishguardbay.com

MAPS
Ordnance Survey Explorer OL35; Landranger 157

As you approach Solva there are fine views to be enjoyed.

Photo: Fiona Barltrop

This is one of the finest of many wonderful coastal walks along the Pembrokeshire coast and it's well served by buses, too, so you can park at St David's, take a bus to Newgale and walk back. By Fiona Barltrop.

❶ **Start**
Alight from the bus at the café at the bottom of the hill just before the bridge. Walk back up hill a short distance and pick up coast path that leaves road on L. Now just keep the sea on your L! Look back for fine views of Newgale Sands. In spring and early summer the clifftops are carpeted by wild flowers, while by late summer/autumn colourful heather and gorse dominate. After passing two notable promontories, Dinas Fawr and Dinas Fach, you may be surprised by a NT sign 'St Elvis',

the name of a nearby farm. Apparently St Elvis was the bishop of Munster in Ireland. Since only 20 miles away to the north are the Preseli Hills, such a coincidence is considered by some as clear evidence that the famous Elvis was of Welsh ancestry! After crossing one last valley you climb up on to the Gribin from where there are excellent view's over Solva's splendid harbour, a favourite with yachties. Once down by the harbour itself you'll pass a number of 18th/19th-century limekilns. The lime was used to fertilise the poor soil of the area.

❷ **6.5km/4 miles**
There are places for refreshment as well as a craft shop, art gallery etc in Solva itself. When you're ready to move on walk down the west

➡

84

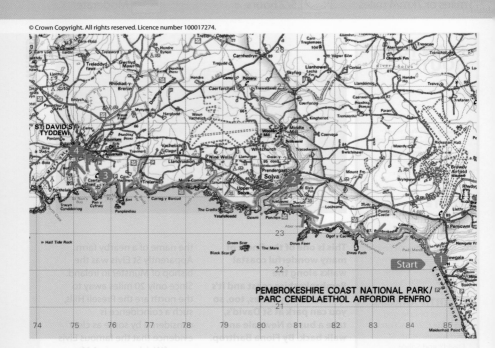

PEMBROKESHIRE COAST NATIONAL PARK/
PARC CENEDLAETHOL ARFORDIR PENFRO

Start

side of the harbour and follow
the coast path signs that direct
you uphill past a few houses
and back on to the clifftop for
an excellent view of Solva's
harbour. As you head west
there are good views towards
distant Ramsey Island. On the
headland between Caerbwdy
and Caerfai Bay is an
impressive Iron Age hillfort.
The beautiful purple sandstone
used for St David's Cathedral
comes from these two bays.

❸ 13km/8½ miles
From Caerfai Bay it's about
1km by road into St David's,
but you could walk on to the
next bay, St Non's, named after
St David's mother. David is said
to have been born on the site
of the ruined chapel here.
There is a holy well and
modern chapel and retreat.
You can take a footpath or the
lane into St David's.

❹ 15km/9½ miles
St David's, Britain's smallest
city, is no more than a village in
size, its cathedral and ruined
Bishop's Palace built in a
hollow below the houses and
shops. As a good pilgrim,
you shouldn't miss a visit to
the cathedral.

13 **Distance** 13km/8 miles	**Time** 4 hours	**Grade** Moderate

WALES

PLAN YOUR ROUTE

ROUTE

Is it for me? Sea cliffs, sand dunes and woodland with several steep climbs
Stiles None
Suitable for children and dogs

START/PARKING

Gower Heritage Centre car park, grid ref SS543892
Nearest town Swansea
Refreshments Shepherds coffee shop in Parkmill; Gower Inn 500m east
Public toilets None
Public transport Bus 114 or 118 from Swansea to Shepherds Parkmill
Accommodation Book a B&B at the 'Book a Bed' section of www.countrywalking.co.uk

MAPS

Ordnance Survey Explorer 164; Landranger 159

Looking over Three Cliffs Bay from Great Tor.

Photo: Tom Bailey

It's a long hike from the car park to Three Cliffs Bay, which may explain why, unlike other Welsh beaches, it's so quiet. But that can only be a good thing. With ruined Pennard Castle perching on the cliff edge, sand dunes and a dramatic beach, this walk has it all. Climbing to the top of Great Tor and the site of an ancient burial chamber, you get stunning views of Three Cliffs and Oxwich Bay. As a cool-down exercise, the walk finishes with a descent through a wooded valley teeming with wildflowers, wild garlic and gentle streams. By Andrew Reid.

❶ Start
From Shepherds coffee shop, cross road to a public footpath sign pointing to Three Cliffs Bay. Follow footbridge over

stream, then turn L. Climb up through woods with stream below you and to R. Turn L to follow sign pointing to Southgate, and continue walking upwards. Continue past white cottages on L until you reach top with golf course, L. Ahead are stunning views of the ruined Pennard Castle, and Three Cliffs Bay. Continue straight along sand path towards castle.

❷ 3km/1¾ miles
Approach Pennard Castle on boardwalk. On L-hand side is a ruined church. Continue through castle ruins, and walk downwards over sand dunes towards a small stream and footbridge. Continue over footbridge and follow sign pointing to Pobbles Beach. Walk up sand dunes on boardwalk, following marker posts to Pobbles Beach. Ahead

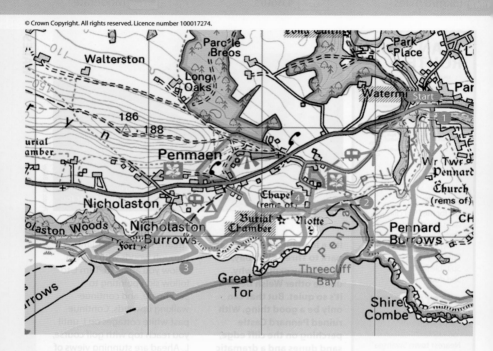

are spectacular views of coastline. Follow marker posts down through dunes to bottom of a valley. Turn R, following marker posts upwards again. Tiny Pobbles Beach is on L. Ahead are triple peaks, which give Three Cliffs Bay its name. At top, turn L and continue along edge of sandy cliff path with beach, L. Descend gently towards to where the beach meets the stony tidemark.

❸ 6km/3¾ miles
Continue straight on to estuary. Cross at stepping stones. Turn L

and follow estuary downstream for a few yards. Ahead are sand dunes of Penmaen Burrows. Leave stream and continue straight through an area of reeds. Follow path upwards through sand dunes towards top of Great Tor cliffs. Follow cliff path with sea, L. At top of Great Tor, there are breathtaking views of Oxwich Bay. Continue following cliff path to a drystone wall. Head R with wall, L. At T-junction, head R over site of ancient burial chamber. Continue along path, descending through sand dunes.

❹ 11km/6¾ miles
Reach bottom of sand dunes. Turn L to path leading steeply upwards. Continue straight on with cottages on L and woods, R. Turn L at public footpath sign. Follow road. Turn R at T-junction. Continue with North Hills Farm, R. Continue straight along track. To R are best views of Three Cliffs Bay. Continue through gate and continue down through woods, which are full of wild garlic in the warmer months. Turn R at road and walk a few yards to Shepherds coffee shop.

FLINTSHIRE
MOEL ARTHUR

Country **walking**

WALES

Distance
12.9km/8 miles

Time
4½ hours

Grade
Moderate

PLAN YOUR ROUTE

The Clwydian Hills offer superb vistas in all directions.

Photo: Steve Goodier

ROUTE

Is it for me? Excellent paths, lots of ups and downs (can be muddy), quiet lanes
Stiles 5
Suitable for fit regular walkers, older children, dogs on leads

START/PARKING

Car park under Moel Arthur, grid ref SJ147657
Nearest town Mold
Refreshments None
Public toilets Mold
Public transport Buses between Mold and Denbigh and Ruthin and Denbigh

MAPS

Ordnance Survey Explorer 265;
Landranger 116

The Clwydian Hills of North Wales are classed as an Area Of Outstanding Natural Beauty and are a spectacular upland region with far-reaching views and a good path network. This walk explores the less popular section of the magnificent Clwydian ridge and visits two ancient hillforts on the summits of Moel Arthur and Penycloddiau, following the line of Offa's Dyke long-distance footpath. There are plenty of ups and downs with superb vistas in all directions. After a high-level jaunt a return is made around the base of the ridge using quiet bridleways high above the Vale of Clwyd.
By Steve Goodier.

❶ **Start**
Leave car park at north-east corner via a wall gap by Moel Famau County Park sign and footpath sign for 'Coed Llangwyfan – 1 mile'. Follow Offa's Dyke long-distance footpath as it climbs up hillside before levelling out and take a clear path L near a gate in wall/fence, R. Climb to summit of Moel Arthur with its cairn and magnificent views. Return same way to rejoin Offa's Dyke at gate and go L, dropping through heather to cross two stiles in quick succession and finally drop steeply on a grassy path to a third stile near a road. Cross over, go R and on reaching road go R and then L to rise into a car park.

❷ 2km/1¼ miles
Still staying with Offa's Dyke path, leave car park at L corner by Penycloddiau Bridleway sign to enter Llangwyfan Forest. Take R fork immediately and then very shortly go R again to follow a rising track through trees (still Offa's Dyke).

Climb steadily to leave trees and enter open ground to rise to a stile and gate. Cross over and climb open hillside on a good path next to a fence, L. When fence drops away, L, stay on main path and keep climbing until you reach hillfort on summit of Penycloddiau.

❸ 3.5km/2¼ miles
Leave summit north-westerly descending through the fort's defence ditches on steps. Continue to a stile, go over and descend long slope on a good path to finally reach a small plantation, R, and drop to a junction of paths near a gate and stile and close to a farm.

❹ 5.6km/3½ miles
Ignore stile and gate and go L on wide track which is a bridleway. This excellent path contours hillside beneath Penycloddiau and gradually drops, taking in some lovely sweeping bends as it does. Pass through six gates to reach a road near houses, R.

❺ 9.2km/5¾ miles
Go L and pass entrance to Llangwyfan Forest, L, and follow road as it bends R to take a bridleway, R. Another excellent track traverses lower slopes of the Clwydian ridge, this time rising gently and passing through eight gates to road. Go L here and walk uphill back to your car.

4.4

Distance
14.4km/9 miles

Time
5 hours

Grade
Moderate

WALES

PLAN YOUR ROUTE

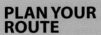

ROUTE
Is it for me? Mainly clear paths, short section on access land, a few steep climbs
Stiles None
Suitable for all, but take care in poor weather – it can be treacherous

START/PARKING
Car park on left between Pontsticill and the Neuadd Reservoirs, grid ref SO037170
Nearest town Merthyr Tydfil
Refreshments None on route
Public toilets None
Public transport None

MAPS
Ordnance Survey Explorer OL12; Landranger 160

Heading up from the Neuadd Reservoirs to the ridgeline.

Photo: Tom Bailey

The Beacons Horseshoe is a gorgeous mountain route – airy and high, yet still very do-able. It takes in the highest point in southern Britain, plus three other tops, but best of all, after a steep puff up at the start, it's ridgeline (with a few rollercoaster dips!) all the way. Great views, minimum effort – it doesn't get much sexier than that. By Jenny Walters.

❶ Start
Leave parking area and turn L along narrow road towards Neuadd Reservoirs. Follow to gate across road by buildings.

❷ 1.3km/¾ mile
Go through gate, down over footbridge and up on to dam wall at end of Lower Neuadd Reservoir. Turn L along wall with views over reservoir and

to Beacons beyond. Bear R at edge of reservoir, then L through trees and head uphill, keeping close to forest on your L. Follow path to ridgeline.

❸ 2.5km/1½ miles
Turn R and follow clear path along ridgeline. There's a precipitous drop on your R so take care in poor visibility. Follow along Graig Fan Ddu, over narrower – but not scary – ridge of Rhiw yr Ysygfarnog and along to junction of paths at Bwlch Duwynt.

❹ 6.3km/4 miles
Turn R and head uphill over peak of Corn Du – or bear slightly further R on path which contours round peak rather than over it. The paths soon join together again. Follow clear path to summit of Pen y Fan.

A great view looking back towards the Neuadd Reservoirs.

❺ 7.3km/4½ miles
From summit, take path R (south-easterly direction) down Craig Cwm Sere to pass. Ignore Beacons Way forking R here and take steep path ahead to summit of Cribyn.

❻ 8.6km/5¼ miles
Ignore steep path to L down snout of Cribyn and follow ridgeline as it curves R along Craig Cwm Cynwyn, dropping gently down to Bwlch ar y Fan. From pass, follow path straight on up to summit of Fan y Big, keeping an eye out for famous Diving Board rock hanging out over the abyss to your L!

❼ 10.3km/6½ miles
From Fan y Big, turn R, heading south to Craig Cwmoergwm. When path begins to swing L, bear R downhill (in a SSW direction) over access land to join clear track to your R, at far end of reservoirs. There are vague sheep tracks, but no clear path and it is boggy in places.

❽ 12.8km/8 miles
Join track and turn R towards reservoir. Turn L on path round buildings and follow road back to car.

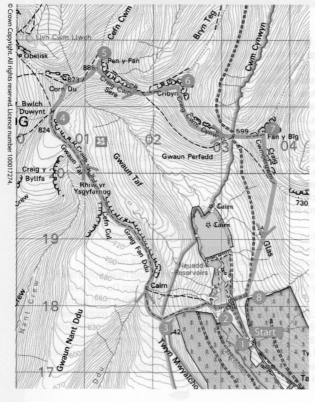

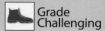
9.8 **Distance** 9.8km/6 miles	**Time** 5 hours	**Grade** Challenging

PLAN YOUR ROUTE

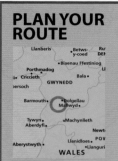

WALES

Heading back down towards Minffordd near the end of the walk.

Photo: Matthew Roberts

ROUTE

Is it for me? Mainly clear paths but rough and rocky underfoot in places; some very steep ascents/descents; route-finding tricky in mist
Stiles 2
Suitable for experienced hillwalkers

START/PARKING

Minffordd car park, grid ref SH731115
Nearest town Dolgellau
Refreshments None on route
Public toilets In car park at start/finish
Public transport Buses X32/32 Bangor – Machynlleth runs through Minffordd (there are two Minffords en route – you want the one south of Dolgellau on A487/B4405 junction)

MAPS

Ordnance Survey Explorer OL23; Landranger 124

Cadair Idris is Wales' most popular peak after Snowdon – and this walk will show you why. The Pony Path from Ty-nant is the easiest ascent, but try this cracking route from the other side – it's worth the extra effort. Head up to the rock-cradled Llyn Cau and then round the rollercoaster ridgeline above. The going can be steep and rocky – but nothing too airy – and the views are quite simply awesome, taking in the Long Mynd of Shropshire, Snowdon, the Rhinogs, Plynlimon, the Lleyn Peninsula and over the sea to Ireland (on a really, really good day). It's magic. Pure and simple. By Jenny Walters.

❶ Start
Go through gate in corner of car park (behind public toilets) signposted 'Cader Idris'. Turn R on Tarmac track, over bridge and up through gate. Follow track as it swings L in front of a building called Ystradlyn, over a stream, then turn R uphill through gate, again signposted for 'Cader Idris'. Follow stepped rocky path steeply uphill through woods, through gate in wall on to access land, and along beside a stream to a path junction.

❷ 900m/½ mile
Take L fork signed 'Cwm Cau' (the R fork is where you come back down). The path swings up round to L, then levels out along the L-hand side of valley towards Llyn Cau. Follow to water's edge, ignoring steep path rising to L.

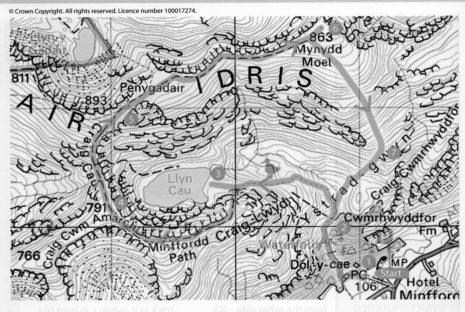

❸ 2.3km/1½ miles
Retrace your steps about 300m and take that steep path (now on R) up to ridgeline – it's hard going but well-built. At pass, turn R to follow path climbing steadily uphill with Llyn Cau dropping away on your R. Keep going on clear route towards the top of Craig Cwm Armach. Be very careful on this section in poor visibility – the drop to the lake is precipitous.

❹ 3.9km/2½ miles
Head over ladder-stile in fence, over peak and downhill to Craig Cau saddle, before climbing up to the summit of

Cadair Idris – aka Penygadair. The path can be a little indistinct at times, but cairns mark the way over steep rocky ground to the triangulation point at the top – and those mind-boggling views.

❺ 5km/3 miles
From summit, follow ridge in an approximately east-north-easterly direction towards Mynydd Moel. The way is clear in good weather but be VERY careful in mist as the drop to the north is sheer. Go over ladder-stile in fence – the peak of Mynydd Moel is just beyond.

❻ 6.8km/4¼ miles
From summit, return to fence and follow it downhill past two ladder-stiles on R – it's steep and grass can be slippery. Keep heading downhill on clear path, following until it swings R over a ladder-stile over a wall.

❼ 8.2km/5 miles
Cross stile and follow path downhill until it swings R over a footbridge and then L to rejoin path you came up earlier. Retrace steps down hill, through two gates to Tarmac track and follow it as it swings L and then R back to car park.

GWYNEDD
CARNEDDAU

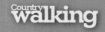
Country **walking**

Distance 14.9km/9¼miles	**Time** 7 hours	**Grade** Challenging

PLAN YOUR ROUTE

Returning to the Ogwen Valley by the shoreline of the Ffynnon Llugwy Reservoir.

Photo: Bob Atkins

ROUTE

Is it for me? Steep paths; two short scrambles (ascent and descent); rocky ridges
Stiles 6
Suitable for fit walkers

START/PARKING

Beside the A5, eastern end of Llyn Ogwen, grid ref SH668605
Nearest town Betws-y-Coed
Refreshments None
Public toilets None
Public transport Snowdon Sherpa bus service connects with most nearby towns, see www.gwynedd.gov.uk

MAPS

Ordnance Survey Explorer OL17; Landranger 115

If you want to challenge your walking skills in Snowdonia, this is the one for you. The Carnedd range includes Pen yr Ole Wen, Carnedd Dafydd, Carnedd Llewelyn and Pen yr Helgi Du, and this route takes in all but the last. It's a magnificent ridge-walk; the bulk of the climbing is done early and the views to Tryfan and the rest of Snowdonia are fantastic. The route is less demanding than the neighbouring Glyderau but due to its length, height of ascent and two tricky steps, it deserves a full summer's day and good navigation skills. By Nick Hallissey.

❶ Start
Cross A5 and follow farm track past Glan Dena cottages, ringed by conifers. Track bends L. Just before gate in wall, turn R on stone path, Afon Lloer

waterfall in view ahead. Cross ladder-stile and follow path marked by stakes. Ford river and continue following staked path L of falls. Cross a further ladder-stile and ascend to Cwm Lloer.

❷ 1.5km/1 mile
Do not approach Ffynnon Lloer tarn, but turn L to face steep ridge curving up to Pen yr Ole Wen. Ridge presents almost solid face, but route up is via a clear scree chute leading to chimney in slabs. Chimney requires three or four scrambled steps, but above this "bad step", path smooths and route clearly follows crest of ridge to summit of Pen yr Ole Wen.

❸ 2.75km/1¾ miles
Turn R on clear path from summit (NNE) to ridge leading to the Carneddau. Pass large

Climbing the Afon Lloer, with Tryfan and the Glyderau in the background.

cairn/shelter at Carnedd Fach and follow ridge to summit of Carnedd Dafydd.

❹ 4.2km/2½ miles
Path veers R (east) – keep to spine of escarpment (Cefn Ysgolion Deon). Ridge continues as Bwlch Cyfryw-drum, terminating in steep ascent to the summit of Carnedd Llewelyn.

❺ 7km/4¼ miles
Turn sharp R, almost back on yourself, to gain path which descends gradually, keeping cliffs of Pen y Waun Wen to L. Path descends to a broad saddle and then to a steep ridge-end, with view of the Eryl Farchog ridge and Pen yr Helgi Du ahead. Descent involves a "bad step" similar to scramble above Ffynnon Lloer. Join Farchog ridge and proceed for 50m, reaching a clear divergence in paths.

❻ 8.2km/5¼ miles
Turn R and follow clear path zig-zagging down flank of ridge. Path reaches shoreline of Ffynnon Llugwy reservoir and continues south to meet old service road. Follow road back down to junction with A5.

❼ 12km/7½ miles
Turn L and follow A5 for 800m to track, R. Follow track to junction with another, R. Take this track and follow west (skirting base of Tryfan) for 2.8km to rejoin A5 at start.

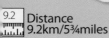 9.2 Distance 9.2km/5¾miles	Time 3 hours	Grade Moderate

PLAN YOUR ROUTE

ROUTE
Is it for me? Riverside paths and clear tracks over open moorland; one steep descent; river section is very rocky and slippery in places
Stiles 2
Suitable for all

START/PARKING
Beddgelert car park, grid ref SH588481
Nearest town Beddgelert
Refreshments Teashops and pubs in Beddgelert
Public toilets Beddgelert
Public transport 97/98/S97 buses run to Porthmadog, Capel Curig and Betws-y-Coed

MAPS
Ordnance Survey Explorer OL17; Landranger 115

Heading up Cwm Bychan after negotiating the Pass of Aberglaslyn.

WALES

Photo: Matthew Roberts

Walking in Snowdonia isn't all high mountains and craggy tops – the rivers, valleys and moors offer spectacular scenery for a lot less sweat. But don't think low-level means dull – this riverside path to the Pass of Aberglaslyn is waterside rock-hopping at its best, and after a relatively gentle ascent, the views from Grib Ddu open into the heart of the Snowdon ranges. By Jenny Walters.

❶ Start
From car park head to main road and turn L. When road bends L over river, take R fork, keeping water on your L. Pass toilets on R, cross footbridge and turn R on to riverside path (water to your R). Follow through two gates to railway line, over tracks (trains still run so take care), then bear L on

path between river and railway. Keep on path as it follows the eastern riverbank – going can be slippery and rocky but there are handholds on the trickier sections – until you see the road bridge at Aberglaslyn.

❷ 2.4km/1½ miles
Bear L uphill just before you reach road, keeping fence on R. Continue through gate in wall, ignore R turn to car park, and go over a railway line (checking for trains again!). Fork L uphill, and follow path up through gates to stone sheepfolds.

❸ 3.8km/2¼ miles
Continue on path as it heads up the rising valley beside a stream and past old mine workings. Ignore fork to L and go straight on uphill and over ladder-stile at the top of Grib

The Fisherman's Path runs right alongside the rushing River Glaslyn – see Point 1.

Ddu – pausing to gawp at the great views. Bear L to path junction with fingerpost.

❹ 5km/3 miles
Turn R downhill on clear track marked 'Llyn Dinas', descending gently at first then more steeply to the shore of the lake.

❺ 6.4km/4 miles
Turn L at lake, go through kissing-gate, then follow path on L-hand side of river, ignoring footbridge to R. Continue on path until you join a road by a bridge, and swing L towards Sygun Copper Mine, turning R just round corner, beyond a stone wall. Take path over field to join narrow road.

❻ 7.5km/4¾ miles
Follow road until it swings R over river, then take footpath over ladder-stile to L and on alongside L-hand side of river. Ignore next bridge to R and continue until you reach the footbridge you crossed at the start. Recross bridge and retrace route back to main road and car park.

GWYNEDD
ARAN FAWDDWY

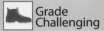
Country walking

| 16.5 | **Distance** 16.5km/10¼miles | **Time** 8 hours | **Grade** Challenging |

PLAN YOUR ROUTE

Looking north from the summit of Aran Fawddwy – Point 4.

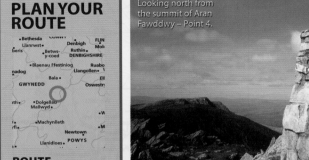

Photo: Laurence Main

ROUTE
Is it for me? Steep mountain paths, grassy track, quiet road
Stiles 6 (ladder-stiles)
Suitable for all who are fit enough

START/PARKING
Llanymawddwy (near telephone box), grid ref SH903190
Nearest town Dolgellau
Refreshments None
Public toilets None
Public transport None

MAPS
Ordnance Survey Explorer OL23;
Landranger 125

Choose a long, sunny day for this most challenging of routes. Wild access land is chosen to approach the 905m peak of Aran Fawddwy – the highest in Britain south of the Snowdon range. By Laurence Main.

❶ Start
With St Tydecho's Church and telephone box R, go L to pass chapel, R, and immediately turn R up signposted path. Climb to ladder-stile, cross it and keep climbing up concrete drive. Just after bearing R with this, turn sharply L to take grassy path. Turn R off this to climb steeply up hillside near a fence, L. Keep near fence on L whilst going over steep hill of Pen Foel y ffridd. Reach a forestry plantation on your L.

❷ 2.8km/1¾ miles
Go left uphill with stream and

forestry plantation L. Climb to wire fence on slope of Drysgol and join well-trodden path up to the Arans (coming from Cwm Cywarch) on its far side, walking with fence R, going uphill.

❸ 4.8km/3 miles
Go ahead over ladder-stile to L of gate. Continue to see lake of Creiglyn Dyfi, source of river, below rocky summit of Aran Fawddwy, R. Take care at Drws bach, the 'little door' to the mountain, marked by a memorial cairn. Walk with fence R and cross ladder-stile in it to keep climbing, fence L. Reach corner formed by summit ridge fence and ignore ladder-stile L. Turn R to ignore another ladder-stile immediately L. Walk with this ridge fence L and ignore another ladder-stile in it. Climb to summit of Aran Fawddwy.

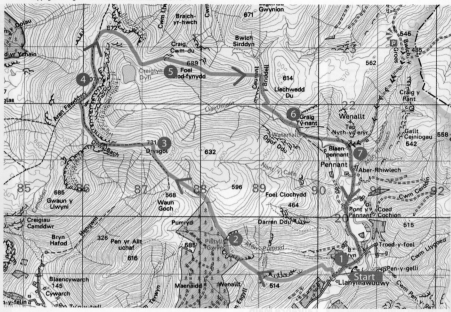

④ 7.2km/4½ miles

With Creiglyn Dyfi below, R, and with Llyn Tegid (Bala Lake) ahead, walk along Arans ridge. Descend, negotiating an old wall, to go ahead across either of two ladder-stiles in fence ahead. Look for gentle, grassy slope R ahead. This is Erw y Ddafad ddu. Turn R down path on Erw y Ddafad ddu, keeping lake of Creiglyn Dyfi away R. Bear L to keep on high ground and reach a corner formed by fencing on Foel Hafod fynydd.

⑤ 9.7km/6 miles

Go ahead with a fence L. Go over brow of hill and descend to stream in Ceunant y Briddell. Step across stream and climb steeply to grassy track. Turn R along this and follow it around a hairpin bend as it descends to overlook the milky infant River Dyfi, R. Approach waterfalls in ravine, R. Divert L here to see a wet depression in a rock called Fynnon Dydecho (Tydecho's Spring) at grid ref SH896217, just above track.

⑥ 12.5km/7¾ miles

Return to track and go down it, above Dyfi, R. Pass a waterfall near a bend, L. Continue with a fence R, going ahead over a ladder-stile. Reach road at foot of Bwlch y Groes.

⑦ 13.7km/8½ miles

Go R down road. Pass Bryn Hall, with its ghosts, before returning to Llanymawddwy. A graveyard of St Tydecho's Church, R, contains bones of Llewelyn Fawr, an 18th-century giant, whilst bones of an ancient giant have been found nearby.

ANGLESEY
HOLYHEAD MOUNTAIN

Country **walking**

9.1	**Distance** 9.1km/5¾miles	
	Time 3½ hours	**Grade** Moderate

WALES

PLAN YOUR ROUTE

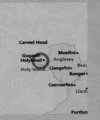

Carmel Head
Gogarth
Holyhead • • Moelfre •
Holy Island • Anglesey
Llangefni • Beau
Bangor •
Caernarfon •
Llanb
Porthm

ROUTE
Is it for me? Good paths throughout; plenty of ups and downs with some rough walking
Stiles None
Suitable for fit walkers with good navigational skills; dogs on lead

START/PARKING
Ynys-Llwd RSPB car park for South Stack Lighthouse, grid ref SH210818 (to visit lighthouse check with Holyhead Tourist Info, tel: 01407 762622
Nearest town Holyhead
Refreshments Main South Stack car park near end of route
Public toilets None
Public transport None to the start

MAPS
Ordnance Survey Explorer 262;
Landranger 114

Looking down over South Stack Lighthouse – see Point 2.

Photo: Steve Goodier

This rough little route explores the wonderful clifftop coast around the puffin sanctuary of South Stack, scrambles over rough ground to the summit of Holyhead Mountain and returns over a rocky headland and mountain terrain. By Steve Goodier.

❶ Start
Leave car park south-westerly picking up Isle of Anglesey Coastal Path. Reach path junction going R along clifftop to Ellins Tower. Pass L, curving R taking steps to lane behind tower. Go L to lane end.

❷ 1km/½ mile
Go through arch and wind down cliff steps (403!) to bridge to South Stack Lighthouse. Return to white arch and go L on Coastal Path, climbing to observation post.

Continue, staying R at path junction and climb to marker post near satellite station. Cross track taking path half-L staying on Coastal Path over crossroads. Go L at path junction and marker post curving L after next marker post staying on Coastal Path and staying R when path splits again, passing another marker post to climb a few steps to path junction, R.

❸ 3.2km/2 miles
Go R climbing rough steps through broken ground to trig on summit of Holyhead Mountain. Leave summit on path north past sign for 'North Stack' descending through steep rough ground to level terrain. Ignore L or R turns and go ahead to climb up North Stack, passing through the old wall to remains of observation post.

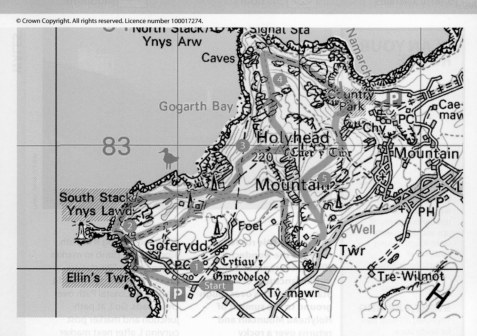

❹ **4km/2½ miles**
Continue ahead to descend on Coastal Path, ignoring any turnings off, to large junction of paths. Fork R joining good track, go R and stay on good track near telegraph line to descend towards car park and lake. As track bends L towards lake take faint path R towards telegraph pole, curving L then R on narrow path that improves at iron fence posts. Climb steeply crossing over path as terrain levels to join better path coming in R. Trend L with path to crossroads, going R to rise short way to join good track at T-junction.

Go R and just before path reaches R side of Holyhead Mountain, take fainter path L, following it under mountainside over rough ground to descend to cross broken wall reaching good path and going R to marker post.

❺ **6.4km/4 miles**
Go L curving to L of quarry to join quarry road. Go L at quarry entrance and continue downhill to join concrete road near reservoirs. Go R, pass barriers and follow road/track to pass reservoir, L, and reach lane end. Take path ahead,

reach marker post and go L with slabs R to climb to another marker post going ahead and ignoring R turn. This path becomes good track passing between satellite station and masts. Ignore L or R turnings and go ahead on good track to pass L of satellite station. At crossroads just after dishes take L fork, following it until just before small road and head down excellent track taking R turn just before gate at track end. Follow path, bear L at next fork, stay L at next fork descending towards South Stack car park to reach lane. Go L up lane back to car park.

POWYS
BLACK MOUNTAIN

Country **walking**

0.6/14.3/10.4

Distance
20.6km/13miles or 14.3km/9 miles
or 10.4km/6½ miles

Time
7/5/3 hours

Grade
Challenging

WALES

PLAN YOUR ROUTE

Reach the shores of Llyn y Fan Fawr at Point 5.

Photo: Britain On View

ROUTE
Is it for me? Moorland paths, indistinct at times and can be rocky underfoot; some long ascents; navigation tricky in bad weather; avoid escarpment edge – drop is sheer in places
Stiles 2
Suitable for fit hillwalkers

START/PARKING
Limited parking east of A4067 opposite turning to Trecastle, close to Tafarn-y-Garreg pub (currently closed), grid ref SN850172
Nearest town Brecon
Refreshments None
Public toilets None
Public transport Veolia Transport Cymru X63 Brecon-Neath Mon – Sat and Beacons Bus B6 and B13 run in the area on Sun. Buses will stop at Tafarn-y-Garreg pub on request

MAPS
Ordnance Survey
Explorer OL12;
Landranger 160

The Carmarthen Fans in the west of the Brecon Beacons offer spectacular hillwalking. After a steep haul up, there's miles of ridgetop walking, with an escarpment plunging to lakes on one side, and a sweep of moorland on the other. The full 20km circuit is a gorgeous day's walk – but long. Divert early for a short loop, or shortly after the high point of Fan Brycheiniog for a medium one. By Jenny Walters.

❶ **Start**
Cross A4067 to car park opposite pub and take track in L corner through gate, over footbridge and through another gate to riverside path. Follow for short distance, then turn L on track uphill with farmhouse on L, bearing R and over stile. Take path straight

ahead uphill, following as it bears R near top to reveal the long ridge of Fan Hir running approximately north. Follow clear path along ridgetop – the drop to your R is sheer so be careful in poor visibility. Continue along ridge to the Bwlch Giedd Pass above Llyn y Fan Fawr.

❷ **5.1km/3¼ miles**
For short loop, turn R on path traversing steeply down south-east to southern shore of lake, then continue route from Point 6. Otherwise, continue on ridgetop path in a NW direction to the triangulation point at Fan Brycheiniog and on to cairn at Fan Foel.

❸ **6.5km/4 miles**
For medium loop, take path north downhill to meet path at base of escarpment, turn R and continue route from Point 5.

Otherwise, follow clear path south-west along ridgeline, down to Bwlch Blaen-Twrch, then uphill to Picws Du. Continue on path round clear ridgeline of Bannau Sir Gaer, following as it curves north above Llyn y Fan Fach. At path junction, fork R down to shore of lake and dam.

❹ 10.7km/6¾ miles
Follow track to north-east, keeping drainage channel R, then bear R towards base of escarpment. Contour round bottom of Picws Du and Fan Foel – path can be indistinct, but stick with base of hills and you should pick it up again.

❺ 13.2km/8¼ miles
Follow base of slope in south-east direction to Llyn y Fan Fawr. Follow path round L-hand side of lake, then bear R along southern shore to base of ridge.

❻ 15.6km/9¾ miles
Take path heading south along base of Fan Hir escarpment (ignore steep path cutting uphill to R). Path can be tricky to spot initially, but becomes clearer, running along a low hill parallel to main ridge. Follow path, over stream, to waterfalls.

❼ 18.5km/11½ miles
Cross stream again and follow path heading along valley. It can be boggy and indistinct, but becomes clearer and rockier later. Follow to stile you crossed on to hill earlier, turn L down track, R along riverbank, over footbridge and cross road back to start.

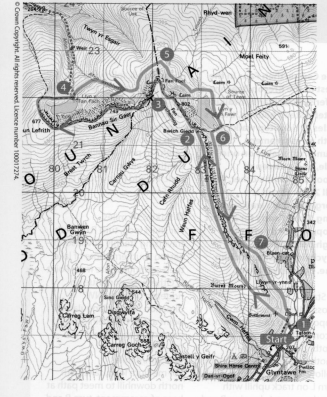

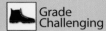
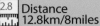

2.8 **Distance** 12.8km/8miles	**Time** 5 hours	**Grade** Challenging

PLAN YOUR ROUTE

WALES

Enjoy great views from the north-east ridge.

Photo: Paul Hannon

ROUTE

Is it for me? Woodland; rough mountain paths; steep mountain ridge with some scrambling (can be avoided); wet patches
Stiles 13
Suitable for experienced, fit hillwalkers

START/PARKING

Capel Curig village car park, grid ref SH720582
Nearest town Betws-y-coed
Refreshments Pinnacle Café, Capel Curig
Public toilets Below car park at start
Public transport Buses from Llanrwst, Betws-y-coed, Bethesda and Porthmadog; trains to Betws-y-coed

MAPS

Ordnance Survey Explorer OL17 & OL18; Landranger 115

Choose a clear, sunny day for this route up isolated Moel Siabod and you will be rewarded with superb, panoramic views of northern Snowdonia's mountains. No other mountain can offer such splendid views of the Snowdon horseshoe whilst to the north are the Glyder range and Carneddau with Tryfan peeping above. To the south, across the Lledr Valley are the hills of southern Snowdonia. By Dorothy Hamilton.

❶ **Start**
From car park turn R through gate and after stile bear L to track that passes behind house. Beyond a gate, it bears L to road. Cross and turn L then climb R-hand stile to have great views of Llynnau Mymbyr and Snowdon. Cross a footbridge and turn L along

track that passes above buildings and goes through woods to a junction. Turn L and ignore L-hand track but go ahead around a barrier. Further on go up steps and beside fence above river. Go slightly R and downhill through trees to riverbank where you bear R to a field. At barn slant R to footbridge then L to a drive and lane.

❷ **3.8km/2½ miles**
Turn R for 100m then go R along wooded lane with a cattle grid. When it bends R go ahead on path marked 'diversion'. Rejoin track above Rhos Farm and walk uphill going over stile with Moel Siabod ahead. Track bends R to a stile then L to next one. Pass a small lake on L and follow rough path uphill, passing a slate tip and ruined quarry buildings. After water-filled pit

Left: The quarry track with Moel Siabod ahead.

on R, go over rise to Llyn y Foel. Keep to R of lake and take path up to foot of Daear Ddu ridge. A steep climb with some scrambling lands you just below summit's trig point. (An alternative route can be taken over grass some distance to L of ridge.)

❸ **8.8km/5½ miles**
After enjoying views take north-east ridge for about 300m. At a flattish, rocky, peaty area, and before a bouldery rise, veer L to pick up a stony path heading in direction of forest east of Llynnau Mymbyr. Partway down mountain you will meet twin stiles and another stile just above forest. Descend a rocky path through heather and trees, crossing two stiles. At R bend, go L on path to track and bear L. After a few paces take R-hand path and ignore paths leading off. It bends L to track near footbridge crossed earlier. Walk up to road and bear R to start.

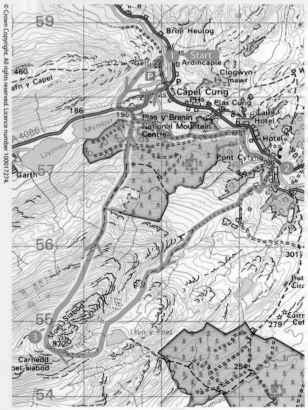

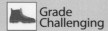
Distance 10.9km/6¾miles	Time 4 hours	Grade Challenging

WALES

PLAN YOUR ROUTE

ROUTE

Is it for me? Woodland and moorland paths with some superb ridge walking
Stiles 6
Suitable for all

START/PARKING

At the foot of Pistyll Rhaeadr, grid ref SJ073295
Nearest town Llanfyllin
Refreshments At start
Public toilets At start
Public transport Bus D76 runs between Welshpool and Llanrhaedr-ym-Mochnant on weekdays. It's 6.4km from there to Pistyll Rhaeadr and timing means you will need to stay overnight

MAPS

Ordnance Survey Explorer 255; Landranger 125

Pistyll Rhaeadr – the highest waterfall in England and Wales.

Photo: Laurence Main

Pistyll Rhaeadr, the highest waterfall south of Scotland, plummets over a cliff to a pool, then tumbles as a narrow spout for a total of 73m (240ft). This makes it higher than Niagara Falls. One of the legendary 'Seven Wonders of Wales', the waterfall is a dramatic prelude to the spectacular 820m (2,700ft) ridge where you overlook a lake. By Laurence Main.

❶ Start
With tearooms L and toilets R, take a gate ahead and bear R to foot of waterfall. Reach footbridge, L, and turn R along signposted path through woodland. Continue through gate on to open hillside and turn L at signposted junction to climb steeply with narrow path. Go L along higher, wider path.

Looking down on valley, L, notice distinctive rocks of Braich y Gawres and Braich y Cawr, glacial erratics deposited in the green meadow. Legend refers to giants dropping them when disturbed building a bridge but the real giant association is in the giant faces they each form. Continue to a waymark post where this wide path starts to swing R. Divert L off it down to gate in wall giving access to top of falls, where children and dogs must be controlled!

❷ 0.8km/½ mile
Retrace steps to waymark post and go L to resume previous direction along wider path. Pass cairn, R, as you walk up valley with River Disgynfa below, L. Go ahead along lower path, pass sheepfold, R. Descend to gate above second sheepfold, L. Step across

stream (Nant Y Cerrig-duon) near its confluence with River Disgynfa, L. Bear R for 200m to pass above small gorge, R, then turn L to aim for cairn. Near this is a stone row and a stone circle. Since these stones are small, they are almost impossible to find when bracken is high. If determined to find them, allow plenty of time! A parish boundary stone for Glan Hafol, dating from 1824, indicates the area.

❸ 2.8km/1¾ miles
Keep ascending to summit ridge and go R with path which is soon accompanied by fence, R. A ladder-stile leads to summit of Moel Sych.

❹ 5.2km/3¼ miles
Take second ladder-stile to continue beside a fence, L, to summit of Cadair Berwyn. You'll know it by its trig point preceded by a pond.

❺ 6.4km/4 miles
Retrace steps from trig point and pass pond away R as you keep closer to edge of cliff, L. Climb to pass a cairn, L. Bear L to descend and pass lake, L. Bear R with path down valley of Nant y Llyn, stream R. Converge with a lower path.

❻ 10km/6¼ miles
Turn R and descend to step across stream, then join another path at hairpin bend. Go L down to signpost for path to top of hairpin bend. Go L down to signpost for path to top of falls ascending steeply, R. Go ahead to retrace steps through woodland to tearooms and car park.

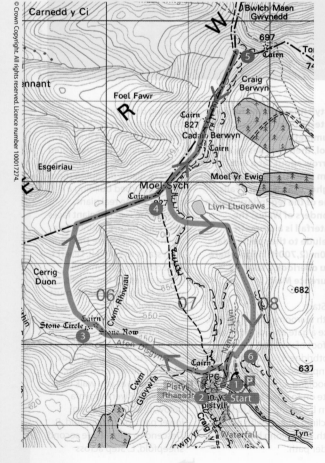

MONMOUTHSHIRE
SUGAR LOAF

Country walking

.6

Distance
6.6km/4miles

Time
3½ hours

Grade
Easy

WALES

PLAN YOUR ROUTE

ROUTE
Is it for me? Good paths throughout with one steep ascent; some rough ground
Stiles None
Suitable for children 7+; dogs on lead

START/PARKING
Viewpoint car park near end of minor road off A40 above Abergavenny, grid ref SO268167
Nearest town Abergavenny
Refreshments Abergavenny
Public toilets Abergavenny
Public transport None to start

MAPS
Ordnance Survey Explorer OL13; Landranger 161

Sugar Loaf is a prominent landmark for miles around.

Photo: Steve Goodier

The Sugar Loaf, or Y Fal, towers over Abergavenny and is a prominent landmark for miles around, looking great from nearly every angle. The name alone will be enough to make your kids up for the ascent, but Sugar Loaf lives up to all it promises with a great summit ridge, superb views and a high starting point to make the ascent that bit easier. The route below gives a good circuit of the hill and even though it is graded 'Easy', the time allotted gives an indication of the terrain. By Steve Goodier.

❶ Start
From car park head north-easterly taking R of two paths to R of prominent hawthorn bush above. Bear R past tree climbing to T-junction of paths. Go L on track, cross two crossroads of paths and at third crossroad go R downhill towards path up Sugar Loaf ahead. Descend steeply to reach stream in bottom of Cwm Trosnant.

❷ 1.2km/¾ mile
Cross stream, continuing uphill on good path to join a stream in a gully, R. Climb good path with stream R. When stream heads R carry on uphill in shallow gully rising to where path comes in L and carrying on. When second path joins L continue uphill steeply heading for rocks on R end of summit ridge. Just before them path bends L, carry on ahead up rocky gully scrambling easily to ridge and going L to walk along summit to trig point.

❸ 2.3km/1½ miles
Head westerly along summit

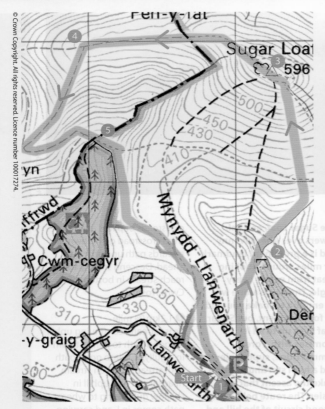

This is a walk all the family will enjoy.

ridge reaching rocks and descend carefully through them to R and drop steeply to join grassy path. Continue along ridge and follow it as it curves L to point where path splits.

❹ 3.7km/2¼ miles Take L fork heading downhill staying R when path splits and descending to a wall, gap and enclosure ahead on fainter path. Go L here to join good path once enclosure, R, ends. Stay by wall on L descending towards plantation to finally leave wall and curve R down to stream by plantation.

❺ 5.3km/3¼ miles Cross stream climbing to stay R at fork and curve R to join wall around plantation. Follow it uphill, go R at corner and follow plantation along to finally climb L and leave wall rising to wall corner. Continue on path next to wall, R, going ahead when path joins L. When wall bends R further on, stay R, keeping near to wall on good track. As wall goes sharp R and path comes in from L, go ahead taking L of two paths (R stays by wall) and leaving wall to cut downhill towards houses on hillside ahead. Descend on good track to car park.

GWYNEDD
NEFYN

Country **walking**

1.5	Distance 11.5km/7¼miles	Time 3½ hours	Grade Moderate

PLAN YOUR ROUTE

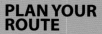

ROUTE

Is it for me? There are no major difficulties, just one short scramble at Point 4
Stiles 5
Suitable for fit walkers

START/PARKING

Car park on the B4417 south-west of town centre, grid ref SH303406
Nearest town Pwllheli
Refreshments The Ty Coch Inn is by the water's edge at Porth Dinllaen and there is a café on the beach towards the end of walk
Public toilets At Porth Dinllaen and at the end
Public transport Four buses a day from Pwllheli (tel: 01286 679535)

MAPS

Ordnance Survey Explorer 253; Landranger 123

Rocky outcrops are characteristic of the first part of the coastal path.

Photo: Len Banister

After visiting the attractive village of Morfa Nefyn and taking in the views of the local mountains, this walk descends to the pretty inlet of Aber Geirch and, after a brief scramble, takes you on to the flower-lined Llyn Coastal Path. The rocky outcrops are replaced by sandy beaches once the point of Porth Dinllaen is passed. By Len Banister.

❶ Start
Go L from car park. Go R along Lon Ty'n Pwll, passing Northern Lights. When lane goes R, keep forward L of gate along R field edge, through gate to pass pond and turn L. Follow slate path to road.

❷ 1.2km/¾ mile
Go R into Morfa Nefyn keeping forward on Aberdaron Road

and passing that to Porth Dinllaen to go R on drive to caravan park. Leave track before buildings to go R alongside wall, through gate along hedged path. Reach kissing-gate.

❸ 3.3km/2 miles
Go L up ladder-stile to go along R field edge. At fence go slightly R to gate then forward to descend to R of bay.

❹ 4.2km/2½ miles
Follow waymarker to scramble up Llyn Coastal Path to stile. Keep L of golf course, following yellow arrows. After 1km, take R fork up to ridge to proceed to lookout.

❺ 6.5km/4 miles
Cross to lifeboat flag and descend by concrete path. Cross sandy bay to steps and

➡

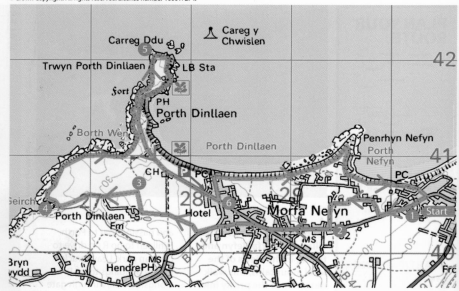

continue along sea edge to Ty
Coch Inn. Go up steps behind
pub and R on drive. At top go L
past clubhouse on road.

❻ 8.3km/5¼ miles
Turn L at first junction through
National Trust car park. Go R at
far end, down steps, across
road, and up again to clifftop,
ignoring R turn. Keep forward
on section of lane and go L at
fingerpost. Go L at building.
There is a single path to the
point. Return taking L fork. At a
metalled lane turn L and go L at
waymarker then L down steps
to beach (you can continue
along clifftop) to road. Follow to
main road and go R at war
memorial to your car.

Mountains and hills form a perfect backdrop.

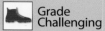

| **Distance** 14.9km/9¼miles | **Time** 5 hours | **Grade** Challenging |

WALES

PLAN YOUR ROUTE

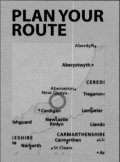

Aberdyfi•

Aberystwyth •

CEREDI
Aberaeron•
New Quay• Tregaron•

•Cardigan Lampeter
ishguard Newcastle Llando
Emlyn
ESHIRE CARMARTHENSHIRE
to Narberth Carmarthen •Lla
•St Clears
• Ar

ROUTE
Is it for me? Clifftop paths, steep in places. Short sections of quiet roads. Suitable for all
Stiles 7

START/PARKING
Llangrannog, grid ref SN311541
Nearest town Aberaeron
Refreshments Llangrannog, Cwmtydu, New Quay
Public toilets Llangrannog, Cwmtydu, New Quay
Public transport It's a two car trail for logistics, unless you go from June to September when the Cardi Bach bus (600) runs between Cardigan and New Quay via Llangrannog and Cwmtydu. Timetable not confirmed at time of going to press.

MAPS
Ordnance Survey Explorer 198; Landranger 145

Approaching Castell Bach from Cwmtydu — see Point 3.

Photo: Laurence Main

**This walk sparkles with vitality, whether it is the dramatic scenery such as the elephant-shaped head and trunk of Pendinaslochdyn and Ynys Lochtyn, the newly excavated Coast Path running along the cliff south of Cwmtydu or the vivacity of New Quay. Dolphins play in the harbour here at high tide. Perhaps they are calling for Dylan Thomas to take to the drink again. Here is the real Llareggub (try spelling that backwards) of 'Under Milk Wood'. Take a tour of the pubs to hear all about the Boyo, starting with Caitlin's favourite Dolau Inn.
By Laurence Main.**

❶ Start
Face sea and go R to pass café on R and climb a steep flight of steps in corner of beach to reach clifftop and follow Coast Path with sea, L. Take a gate to converge with a grassy track and go L. Follow path as it sweeps around hillside which is crowned by an ancient hillfort up on R. The land slopes down to island of Ynys Lochtyn, L. Keep above sea on your L.

❷ 1.6km/1 mile
Go ahead over a stile, then a second stile. Ignore kissing-gate, R. Overlook Urdd Gobaith Cymru (Welsh League of Youth) Centre. Descend to a signpost and go L beside a fence on R. Turn R at next

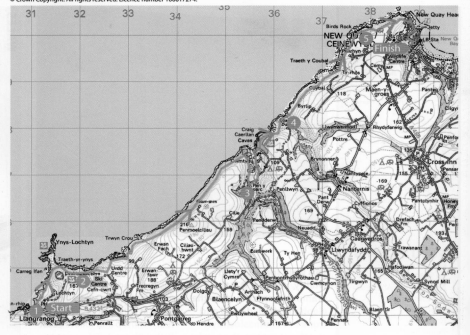

signpost. Take a kissing-gate and walk with a fence, L. Ignore a signpost path going inland on R. Keep sea L and proceed to newly created path leading to Cwmtydu. This is a tremendous walk along side of a steep cliff. Incredibly, an excavating machine dug the path. Whoever drove it had nerves of steel! Turn R at a signpost and descend through woodland to a road.

❸ 7.2km/4½ miles
Go L down road, cross a bridge and go L to reach Cwmtydu.

Walk with cove L and limekiln R. Climb with a path from corner of beach and go L with signposted 'Coast Path', keeping sea L. Pass through prehistoric promontory fort of Castell Bach.

❹ 9.7km/6 miles
Cross footbridge in Cwm Soden and climb to a signpost junction. Go L with Coast Path. Keep sea L as you cross footbridges and stiles above beach of Traeth Y Goubal.

❺ 12km/7½ miles
Pass a lookout shelter, L. This is above Birds Rock. Follow Coast Path to see New Quay on R, before descending to Lewis Terrace. Turn L down a signposted path to reach old quarry, where Llareggub's Mr Waldo carried on with Mrs Beattie Morris. Descend to fish-processing factory and go R along Rock Street to reach tourist information centre and harbour. Go R up Church Street to pass Dolau Inn, R. Turn L along Hill Street (which becomes Park Street) to find bus stop.